A Late Encounter with the Civil War

E S T. 75 1 9 3 8
YEARS
THE UNIVERSITY OF GEORGIA PRESS 2013

Mercer University Lamar Memorial Lectures No. 55

A LATE ENCOUNTER WITH THE CIVIL WAR

MICHAEL KREYLING

THE UNIVERSITY OF GEORGIA PRESS   Athens and London

© 2013 by the University of Georgia Press
Athens, Georgia 30602
www.ugapress.org
All rights reserved
Set in Sabon and ITC Century by Graphic Composition, Inc.
Printed and bound by Sheridan Books, Inc.
The paper in this book meets the guidelines for
permanence and durability of the Committee on
Production Guidelines for Book Longevity of the
Council on Library Resources.

Printed in the United States of America

13 14 15 16 17 P 5 4 3 2 1

Library of Congress Cataloging-in-Publication Data

Kreyling, Michael, 1948–
A late encounter with the Civil War / Michael Kreyling.
pages cm. — (Mercer University Lamar memorial lectures ; No. 55)
Includes bibliographical references and index.
ISBN 978-0-8203-4619-9 (hardcover : alk. paper) —
ISBN 0-8203-4619-5 (hardcover : alk. paper) —
ISBN 978-0-8203-4657-1 (pbk. : alk. paper) —
ISBN 0-8203-4657-8 (pbk. : alk. paper)
1. United States—History—Civil War, 1861–1865—Centennial celebrations, etc.
2. United States—History—Civil War, 1861–1865—Historiography.
3. Collective memory—United States. I. Title.
E641.K74 2013
973.7—dc23   2013021449

British Library Cataloging-in-Publication Data available

Contents

꒰꒱

Preface

꙳

While I was revising the lectures that would become the basis for this book and my visit to Mercer University in October 2012, I was living on the coast of California, about 120 miles north of San Francisco. It was summer, not a summer of the Deep or the Middle South that I knew but a summer of Sonoma County, California, which I had not known or even imagined. As a natural place, the Sonoma coast is geological rather than historical: steep and rocky bluffs above the Pacific, audible breaking seas all day long (especially at night) as much as a mile up the redwood and fir slopes. Russians lived there until gold fever hustled them out. They left a small settlement called Fort Ross and a river called the Russian River, known these days less for the ousted colonizers who traded in seal and sea otter pelts and more for its mellow pinot noirs. In other words, if the ground I lived on was even remotely "dark and bloody," the American Civil War had no part—the battles had not swept across or even near the Sonoma coast.

In July the California Historical Artillery Society sponsored Civil War Days in Duncans Mills, a small railroad depot town (population 85) near the mouth of the Russian River, which had remained unsettled until the 1870s. Despite the town's noninvolvement in the Civil War, Blue and Gray reenactors fired upon one another at a campground near the river in two mock engagements per day on Saturday and Sunday. When I arrived on the Sunday, the score was Blue: 2, Gray: 0, but the host and master of ceremonies said he expected the series to even up. Between battles the "behind the lines" encampments were open for Civil War cookery demonstrations, weaponry exhibits, tool displays, and horse pettings.

By the time I left Sunday afternoon, the final score was Blue: 3, Gray: 1. The whiffs of gunpowder and cannon smoke had cleared from the pristine blue sky; the concussions of cannons were replaced by the roars of Harley Davidsons as the motorcycle clubs wheeled out, and the Civil War seemed, among these surroundings of ocean, river, vineyards, and temperate sunshine, about as accessible through memory as the Punic Wars. Wouldn't a "real" battlefield be a better venue for thinking about our American Civil War a century and a half after it happened? I don't think so.

This book began before the invitation from the Lamar Lectures Committee arrived. For a couple of years, I had been thinking about what we do to the past when we remember it and what kind of experience of the past memory is, and at the advent of the Civil War Sesquicentennial these thoughts focused the generalized "past" into "Civil War." As a nation we had formally and publicly undertaken commemorations of the whole war at least twice before—for the fiftieth anniversary, the semicentennial, and for the one hundredth, the centennial—where historians and cultural studies critics had examined these rituals of memory and nationhood, providing a conversation to listen to and, in the end, to join.[1] The ticket for joining the conversation on cultural, collective, or public memory is not acquired easily or quickly; even with this book my ticket does not begin at the beginning and take me all the way to the end. But certain people in the field have been the source of basic, shaping concepts, and by way of introduction, I briefly outline those concepts here.

The study of collective, social, or cultural memory (the phenomenon goes by several names) is a mature academic field. Most who work in the field acknowledge Maurice Halbwachs (1877–1945) as the founder, and his posthumous *La mémoire collective* (1950) as the foundational text. Halbwachs was a student of sociologist Emile Durkheim, from whom he absorbed and refined the concept of "collective memory," the premise being that humans assemble or construct memory in the context of social life: we remember what our social groups require us to remember in order to maintain historical continuity over time and to claim our membership in them. Halbwachs's cultural and historical territory was French national and cultural identity; he studied texts, monuments, and patriotic rituals undertaken in the service of French national identity. Much of Halbwachs's work was done in the 1920s and 1930s, the same decades when southerners of various temperaments on this side of the Atlantic ("conservative" Agrarians at Vanderbilt and "liberal" sociologists clustered mainly in and around the University of North Carolina in Chapel Hill) took on the construction, or at least the consolidation, of southern identity in works like the Agrarians' *I'll Take My Stand* (1930) and the sociological journal *Social Forces*, inaugurated in 1922 by Howard W. Odum at UNC–Chapel Hill.

Pierre Nora has extended, and in a sense completed, Halbwachs's project in his seven-volume work *Les lieux de mémoire* (1984–92). His larger argument is distilled in "Between Memory and History: *Les Lieux de Mémoire*."[2] Nora deals chiefly with French collective memory and the means of its transmittal, but two sentences in his *Representations* article concerning New World cultural memory (or, in his opinion, the dearth of it) snagged my attention: "In the United States, for example, a country of plural memories and diverse traditions, historiography is more pragmatic. Different interpretations of the Revolution or of the Civil War do not threaten the American tradition because, in some sense, no such thing exists—or, if it does, it is not primarily a historical construction" (10). These essays came about, in large part, to prove Pierre Nora wrong.

The deep, and contested, hold of memory on southern identity is crucial to understanding the chapters that follow, and I have relied on the work of several contemporary historians who study this phenomenon. W. Fitzhugh Brundage connects the general pursuits of memory studies with the particular aptitude of southerners for it in *Where These Memories Grow: History, Memory, and Southern Identity* (2000).[3] "Southerners, after all," he writes, "have the reputation of being among the most historically oriented of peoples and of possessing the longest, most tenacious memories" (2). And Brundage adds another turn that is just as crucial: "Each time a tradition is articulated, it must be given a meaning appropriate to the historical context in which it is invoked. For a historical memory to retain its capacity to speak and mobilize its intended audience, it must address contemporary concerns about the past" (9–10). This is a more elaborate version of William Faulkner's enigmatic words in *Requiem for a Nun* (1950): "The past is never dead. It isn't even past."[4] Faulkner's line implies that memory haunts southern identity like the Dementors in a Harry Potter novel. But Brundage's touch is lighter, suggesting that memory is not a pall or dead zone but rather a communal event or space, a periodic or ongoing *lieu de mémoire*—a spirit I have attempted to carry over into this book.

In the connected fields of Civil War memory, history, and race politics in the United States, the work of David W. Blight is unavoidable. His two books *Race and Reunion: The Civil War in American Memory* (2001) and *American Oracle: The Civil War in the Civil Rights Era* (2011) are required reading.[5] The earlier of the two explores the era of the semicentennial of the Civil War, and the latter focuses on the centennial. His premise is that Civil War memory and race in American national identity operate on the same political current; in those *lieux de mémoire* where Americans profess to be honoring or revisiting the epic of a national civil war, they are defining their racial politics in whatever present they inhabit. Blight's conclusions are nigh indisputable for the semicentennial and the centennial, but the sesquicentennial, the 150th anniversary, seems to present a cultural climate different in degree and kind. The third chapter of this book addresses this difference: Is there a shelf life to the influence of the past in the present? In an era of Photoshop and computer-generated simulations of experience where we can create a simulacrum of the past indistinguishable from the real thing, which of the several pasts we can conjure do we remember?

"Different traditions of . . . the Civil War" *do* "threaten the American tradition"; as you will read in the second chapter, Robert Penn Warren claimed that differences in interpreting the Civil War *are* the American tradition. The first two official commemorations of the War, its semicentennial and its centennial, amply prove Warren's point. During the sesquicentennial, the question is still open.

A question not open is my debt to many who have helped me clarify and organize my thinking on this topic. Vanderbilt University undergraduates in American Studies 100w ("Memory and the Civil War") endured an early phase of the process during the spring semester of 2011 and survived more or less unscathed (I hope). That same semester another class of Vanderbilt students campaigned through a course on remembering the Civil War, which I team-taught with historian Richard Blackett. To Richard I owe crucial extensions of my knowledge of the Civil War as a real event—the constellation of the material that never gets wholly remembered—and I thank him for his bemused tolerance of my interest in the counterfactual versions of the war. In the early stages of writing the essays I was the invited "scholar" for the Brentwood (Tennessee) Library's program of public discussions of the Civil War: *Let's Talk About It: Making Sense of the American Civil War*, funded by the National Endowment for the Humanities and the American

Library Association. My thanks to the organizer, Robin Zandi, and the dozens of local library-goers who set aside five weekday evenings early in 2012 for reading and discussion of the war and its meaning for the United States in the present century. Special gratitude to the Lamar Lectures Committee for their invitation and to Sarah Gardner, Doug Thompson, and David Davis of Mercer University's Southern Studies program for taking care of me in Macon when I delivered the lectures in October 2012. Thanks to Rebecca Norton and the rest of the staff of the Press for seeing the manuscript through editing and production. As always, to my wife Chris who read every word and made the whole thing better than I ever could have on my own. And for Opie, who walked me through it all.

Michael Kreyling
August 2013
The Sea Ranch, California

A Late Encounter with the Civil War

CHAPTER ONE

Remembering the Civil War in the Era of Race Suicide

We use personal and collective memory of the past to help us negotiate the present, to determine who we are by reminding ourselves of who we have been. And those who study both types of memory tell us that we are used by these negotiations as much as we use them. My focus here is what can be referred to as collective, civic, or ritualized memory—rather than personal, although analogies connect the two. I think of it as a kind of complicated puppet theater; we are the pullers of the strings (insofar as we set dates for ceremonies of public memory and fill the ceremonies with choreographed activities) and the figures pulled. Perhaps not so clearly in the moment, but with enough distance, we can see how the puppeteering works in making our public history address anxieties that consume us in the present. Americans have had, now in the twenty-first century, three large, organized public encounters with our collective memory of the Civil War. The first two are sufficiently distant from us in time that we can see how the string-pulling works, how conscious intentions and unconscious anxieties share the memory space. I propose, by way of these essays, to analyze our two previous commemorations for embedded conscious and unconscious themes and then to project the results on the present, the age of the sesquicentennial. We should then be able to frame the essential questions growing from rituals of collective memory: Are we the same people in all the same ways as our predecessors? Does our distance in time from the event place limits on the effectiveness of public memory?

During the fiftieth anniversary of the war, the semicentennial (1911–15), William Howard Taft (a Republican from Ohio) and Woodrow Wilson (a Democrat from Virginia—the first southerner to sit in the White House since Andrew Johnson) were presidents. The "separate but equal" racial doctrine of *Plessy v. Ferguson* (1896) was the law of the land, and the NAACP was in its first decade of pubic advocacy for the "colored people" whose rights as citizens had been promised after the war but not yet delivered in full. One of the NAACP's first causes was the banning of D. W. Griffith's 1915 film *The Birth of a Nation* (originally titled *The Clansman*), adapted from Thomas F. Dixon's novel *The Clansman* (1905). Race was much on the nation's mind during the semicentennial. The celebration of the fiftieth anniversary of the war occurred during a time when the lynching of African American men was common, particularly in the South. Federal antilynching laws were repeatedly introduced and passed by the U.S. House of Representatives but blocked by southern Democrats in the Senate. The agitation for and against antilynching laws was not exclusively legal but still managed to unlock subconscious anxieties that underlay the discourse of race. Jack Johnson, a black man who had married three white women and defeated the "great white hope" Jim Jeffries in 1910, was convicted of violating the Mann Act in 1913. Rather than serve a prison sentence on the trumped-up charge (Johnson was married to the woman he was accused of transporting across state lines), Johnson left the country. In the wake of the national uproar, a Georgia congressman introduced an amendment to the Constitution forbidding intermarriage between "negros or persons of color and Caucasians."

The proposed amendment failed, but white anxiety over the

mixing of race, blood, and intimate partners prevailed, giving a spin to themes of gendered identity and romantic plots that we might, today, see as obsessive or even hysterical. Widespread anxiety about blood—in its scientific discourse and in its looser cultural one—pervaded the turn of the century and influenced the way the Civil War would be commemorated. Much of this conversation was shaped by Englishman Francis Galton (1822–1911), remembered mostly for his pioneering work in the forensic science of fingerprinting and for his speculations on blood and hereditary racial characteristics for individuals and societies, known as eugenics. In the essay "Blood-Relationship," published in *Nature* (U.K.) in 1872, Galton (Charles Darwin's cousin), asserted a position that became a basis for racial anxiety. "Therefore," Galton calmly asserted, "each individual may properly be conceived as consisting of two parts, one of which is latent and only known to us by its effects on his posterity, while the other is patent and constitutes the person manifest to our senses" (173). Skin color, of course, has always been the principle characteristic of race "manifest to our senses." But Galton suggests that there is a secret sharer of manifest identity—a latent racial identity undetected by the senses and visible only in "posterity." Acts of procreation, insofar as they produce posterity, constitute a racial lottery; if not controlled, unwanted results might appear in human offspring. "Reversion" was always a possibility in the conception of any child of parents of different races, no matter how similar "manifest" racial type might appear to be. Love and marriage, as the lyricist Sammy Cahn wrote, might go together like a horse and carriage, but Galton advised keeping the horse (racial and social purity) before the cart (intermarriage)[1]:

> The observed facts of Reversion enable us to prove that the latent elements must be greatly more varied than those that are personal or patent. The arguments are as follows:—

(1) There must be room for very great variety, because a single strain of impure blood will reassert itself after more than eight generations; (2) an individual has 256 progenitors in the eighth degree, if there have been no ancestral intermarriages, while under the ordinary conditions of social and neighborly life, he will certainly have had a considerable, though a smaller, number of them; (3) the gradual waning of the tendency to reversion as the generations increase, conforms to what would occur if each fresh marriage contributed a competing element for the same place, thus diluting the impure strain until its relative importance was reduced to an insignificant amount. (173–74)

Fear of "reversion" causes anxiety that whiteness will become its Other if, "as the generations increase," variety in intermarriages is not controlled. In places where the eye cannot see (Galton located the main one in the "structureless ovum"), there are a certain finite number of genetic "places" for which elements of pure and impure blood compete (174). Unless these places are reserved for pure blood, "a single strain of impure blood will reassert itself after more than eight generations."

Galton's eugenicist drama of blood influenced the age's thinking and, in turn, the shape of its romances—its love and marriage plots. Probably the most widely known example of the mixture of blood science (or pseudoscience) with the romance of blood is not an American Civil War story but Bram Stoker's vampire classic *Dracula* (1897). The romance in *Dracula* turns on two poles of the meaning of blood articulated by Galton, the clinical or scientific blood that is evident to our senses (and manifestly appalling since blood is best when it is unseen) and the latent symbolic or cultural blood that invades or pollutes the endangered citadel of whiteness. In one crucial *Dracula* scene these two meanings of blood collide. I have in mind the scene in which Dr. Van Helsing determines that Lucy Westenra, inexplicably wasting away with symptoms that suggest potentially fatal anemia, requires a transfusion to save her life. Van Helsing first selects Jack Seward, one of the unsuccessful suitors for Lucy, to be the donor. But when Arthur Holmwood— Lucy's chosen fiancé, a titled and wealthy (white) male—appears, Van Helsing sends Seward to the bench. Holmwood's "blood" (typing or "cross-matching" of actual blood would not become scientific practice for another five years) is deemed more appropriate because, Van Helsing seems to think, "the brave lover" whom Lucy has already chosen can donate a liquid more regenerative than the suitor she has rejected. By setting up the transfusion this way—typing and cross-matching for cultural characteristics rather than for scientific ones—Stoker suggests that blood is not anonymous and universal, as scientific research would soon reveal, but, as Galton theorized, particular to class, racial, and personal characteristics. In *Dracula* readers are prompted to interpret the personal as the cultural. Lucy's family name, Westenra, suggests that she might represent the cherished womb of Western civilization, which, as Galton also theorized, houses a finite number of "places" where the racial script is imprinted. The reader knows, as Van Helsing and his band of Anglo-Saxon brothers do not, that the script has already been "corrupted" by the Count, Vlad the Impaler, the invader from the nebulous land far to the east. Certainly, in this register, Count Dracula represents the threat of "reversion," a racially tainted infusion, and Holmwood's blood the defense mounted by the apex of European civilization.

Van Helsing officiates at the transfusion as he would at a wedding, granting Holmwood one kiss before the transfer and an extra kiss when the procedure is concluded. Readers of *Dracula* already know that Lucy is a creature of the Count before the transfusion and that Arthur Holmwood's "blood," no matter how Anglo-Saxon and aristocratic, will not abolish the taint of the invader. Stoker nevertheless dramatizes the transfusion as a nuptial ceremony, the tubes that join Holmwood's veins to Lucy's awkwardly serving to symbolize the marriage bond.[2]

This scene from *Dracula* shows how cultures shape imagination and memory by attaching threads of concern to creative acts like writing and reading as well as to more conscious expressions in genres like Francis Galton's early eugenicist essays. In the case of blood, the symbolic meaning of the actual fluid precedes developing scientific knowledge and holds its ground against the scientific position.

This is to say, in brief, that the United States that formally remembered the Civil War at the semicentennial was different from the America of the centennial and sesquicentennial by one very powerful theme we can identify in retrospect: blood. By following the theme of blood with specialized attention, we can see how a metaphor controlled conscious meaning.

The intertwined themes of blood and race should be easy to follow. Our national remembering in the era of the semicentennial made conscious, if often just partially conscious, a range of racial anxieties for which blood served as the central metaphor. One conscious manifestation of Anglo-Saxon racial anxiety was summed up in a phrase that echoed across the era: "race suicide." The decades leading up to the semicentennial—and leading away from the great expenditure of blood in the actual Civil War—were fraught with this Anglo-Saxon anxiety. F. Scott Fitzgerald, a decade after the semicentennial, ridicules this strain of race anxiety in *The Great Gatsby* (1925) when Tom Buchanan—as white a bully as there is—blusters about the rising tide of inferior races in the middle of a conversation about his young daughter.[3] There is little coincidence in Fitzgerald costuming Tom as a buffoonish caricature of Rough Rider Theodore Roosevelt:

He had changed since his New Haven years. Now he was a sturdy, straw-haired man of thirty with a rather hard mouth and a supercilious manner. Two shining arrogant eyes had established dominance over his face and gave him the appearance of always leaning aggressively forward. Not even the effeminate swank of his riding clothes could hide the enormous power of that body—he seemed to fill those glistening boots until he strained the top lacing, and you could see a great pack of muscle shifting when his shoulder moved under his thin coat. It was a body capable of enormous leverage—a cruel body. (12)[4]

There is even less coincidence when, a few pages later, Tom garbles the eugenicist credo that Roosevelt upheld as a matter of private and public policy: " 'This idea is we're Nordics. I am, and you are, and you are, and—' After an infinitesimal hesitation he included Daisy with a slight nod, and she winked at me again. '—And we've produced all the things that go to make civilization—oh, science and art, and all that. Don't you see?' " (17). There are four adults in the room, and the only one whose racial provenance Tom is in doubt about is his wife, the southern girl from Louisville. His bluster confirms the widespread anxiety about race purity, and his "infinitesimal hesitation" slyly insinuates anxiety in the southerness of the blood and breeding theme—as if just the slightest residue of "reversion" hysteria in Tom's muscle-bound Nordic brain surfaces when turning to the South.

Theodore Roosevelt was a vocal spokesman and example of Anglo-Saxon concern about the same issues over which the fictional Tom Buchanan stumbles. Roosevelt summed them up under the heading "race suicide." In a speech to the National Congress of Mothers in 1905, Roosevelt, president of the United States at the time, warned against the popularity of childless marriages and labeled family planning (limiting the number of offspring to two was his example) as "race suicide."[5] What gave marriage, families, and fertility weight for Roosevelt and his audience was the shared anxiety that the supremacy of white "blood" might be inundated by a "rising tide of color." Historians of Theodore Roosevelt and his age agree that his invocation of the rhetoric of "blood" signified a concern about inheritable traits, inclinations, and tendencies that marked racial groups and, more importantly, stacked them in a pyramid from inferior people of color at the base to superior whites at the pinnacle. Not all "blood" was the same. White or European "blood," as Roosevelt was also to pronounce, had rightfully dominated the history of the West for the past four hundred years but was facing a competitive challenge in the new, twentieth century. The challenge came not so much from the quality of the civilizations of colonial peoples and other immigrant populations, which were inferior to the European and lacked the power to supplant them, but from their sheer numbers. "Of course the best that can happen to any people that has not already a high civilization of its own," President Roosevelt proclaimed in a 1909 speech, "is to assimilate and profit by American or European ideas."[6] But if the white birth rate were to decline, or even remain steady, assimilation of non-European peoples might undermine white civilization. Without vigorous and supervised breeding (not love, a less predictable human activity), the "infinitesimal hesitation" of Tom Buchanan might become full-blown doubt. Thus, what might be an expository point in a speech becomes in a novel like *The Great Gatsby* a theme. When Fitzgerald presents Tom Buchanan, adulterer, father of only one child, host to Nick Carraway and Jordan Baker (an infertile couple if there ever was one) blustering about the whiteness of (almost) everyone in the room, the irony resonates well beyond one novel, even backward in time more than a decade before its publication to the years of the semicentennial.

Scientific progress in understanding blood also gave the turn-of-the-century public reason to think about its meanings.

Medical journals such as *JAMA* and the *New England Journal of Medicine* frequently carried, in the years surrounding the semicentennial, the professional medical community's diagnosis of the problem of race decline or "suicide." Declining white birthrates in European nations such as France caused alarm, especially in the United States where immigration from Asia and from the regions of southern and eastern Europe (Dracula's homeland) had become a political issue. Powerful voices like Theodore Roosevelt's called on white women to seek marriage and motherhood; in his speech to the National Congress of Mothers, Roosevelt used the bully pulpit to chastise novelist Robert Grant for his *Unleavened Bread* (1900), a story about a married woman who chooses social advancement over domestic bliss and children.[7] Even women with less selfish agendas than the central character of *Unleavened Bread* were conscripted into the birthrate campaign. Coeducation for women in the United States was flagged as an omen of race suicide, for it was seen to cause a diminution of the "natural" desire for motherhood. So pervasively was race anxiety linked to the body of the white woman, for example, that excessive bicycle riding was suspected of contributing to low fertility. Such peripheral information is relevant to a backward look at the fiftieth anniversary of the Civil War because literary manifestations of that commemoration (novels, plays, films) almost universally include a courtship and marriage plot, and on the darker side a rape threat, that connect the vicarious romantic pleasures of the text with controversial issues of public policy well beyond it.

At the same time that the widespread attention to and anxiety about marriage and procreation used the language of blood (inasmuch as "blood" could be read as an interchangeable metaphor for race or genealogy or social class), blood itself, the actual fluid pumped by the heart through human veins and arteries, also received new and heightened attention. "Nordic" expansion into the equatorial regions—U.S. adventures in Central America and the Philippines, for example—accelerated fears of race suicide and vulnerability since Anglo-Saxon blood seemed (as anecdotal evidence outstripped scientific data) particularly attractive to tsetse flies, assassin bugs, mosquitoes, and other blood-sucking allies of the colonial peoples whose inferior "blood" European civilization (to echo Roosevelt) was destined to improve. Some races thrived in tropical climates but they were darker, and it would have been a severe blow to the theory of European superiority if something as simple as an insect bite could negate the superiority of Western blood.

The age's pervasive fear of race suicide had many branches: the growth of the "science" of eugenics, state and federal immigration laws, laws against miscegenation, Jim Crow segregation, and legal sterilization of mental "defectives" (upheld as legal by the U.S. Supreme Court in *Buck v. Bell* [1927]). But one image seems to have been common to all of the branches: blood. What American and European civilizations were learning about blood, coupled with what they believed about the metaphorical evocations of "blood," shaped rites of commemoration of the Civil War when the fiftieth anniversary arrived. What I would like to do is turn the inside processes outward by focusing attention on a few ways the meanings of blood powered the workings of the American imagination when it brought the Civil War forward for reconsideration.

First, if "race suicide" was a powerful metaphor of the age, reimaginings of the Civil War introduced that metaphor in powerful but subliminal ways during the semicentennial. If the white population of the United States, in some important but not-quite-conscious compartment of its psyche, was as anxious as Tom Buchanan about rising above a tide of color, then the reaction to the commemoration of the deaths of more than six hundred thousand of its males would have elicited, at the least, a subliminal shiver. Killing six hundred thousand of its own potential breeders while freeing approximately four million people of color is alarming cultural arithmetic. In *War's Aftermath: A Preliminary Study of the Eugenics of War* (1914), written just after the war in the Balkans had broken out but before it became a wider European war in August 1914, David Starr Jordan and Harvey Ernest Jordan used the dread of that European war ("that delayed Teutonic migration known as the Great War" according to an ironic Nick Carraway [9]) to assess "the effects, on the Southern States of our National Union, of the reversal of selection due to the loss of life in the Civil War of fifty years ago" (v).[8] To the Jordans, the loss of white males in Confederate armies ("Of the colored or negro population no account is taken in the present discussion" [4]) posed "the theoretically inevitable deterioration due to the loss of a large portion of the best young blood of fifty years ago" (7). The "thoroughbreds of the coming generation" (20), thus removed from the breeding pool, left superior females bereft of "superior males" with the result that southern women "frequently do not marry, or are compelled to marry poorer strains" (47). Romance plots, then, take on the ominous tones of civilization's twilight, and courtship is less personal than racial. "[C]ould we have had the inspiring presence and wise counsel of these martyrs and their potential offspring," the Jordans lament, "the country would now be immeasurably better off in a yet higher average of physical, mental, and moral stamina" (78–79). The number, brutality, and waste of military deaths in the Civil War, framed as they were by such an apocalyptic, eugenicist anxiety, would need to be mitigated or transformed from a narrative of white race suicide into a narrative of interregional (but exclusively white) regeneration. The birth of a nation was the master metaphor of the Civil War semicentennial, simultaneously simplistic and complicated because it was fashioned out of romantic cliché as an antidote to eugenicist doom.[9]

Experimental progress in the science of blood tended to undermine the cultural habit of thinking of blood as specific to different world civilizations and races, and therefore as unmixable. In a laboratory or hospital, human blood could be classified into types, but it still took an act of cultural belief to see red blood as white or black. The gradually emerging scientific knowledge of the interchangeability of blood across racialized groups paradoxically contributed increased stridency to the theme of the disasters of mixing. The general American public at the time of the fiftieth anniversary of the Civil War was still locked into thinking of the bloods of the white and black races as unmixable—that is, unmixable without negative effects for the superior white blood. Americans continued to read "blood" as the sign of all they did not know or see and could not control about the way the human body lives and procreates. Skin color, of course, is all we see—often all we can know—of the race of the body. But when races mix sexually, the color of the skin can become an unreliable sign of racial identity. As Francis Galton had averred many years earlier, manifest signs might indicate white identity while latent forces were rife with impurities that could become manifest on the body in any future generation. Racially mixed characters, then, function as the crowded intersection of cultural anxiety about racial identification and the power that accompanies superior status. The very appearance of the mixed race individual signifies, first, the breakdown or violation of racial purification campaigns, and second, the fear that "blood" might be exposed as a pseudoscientific myth and therefore an unreliable symbol for racial difference and superiority.[10]

Race and blood were significant for the formalized memory of the Civil War at the semicentennial because they dominated ritualized recall of the war's meanings. Like the First World War it foretold, the American Civil War presented the American public with actual blood on a scale we did not, at the time, have narrative shapes to hold. That is one reason Walt Whitman, who visited battlefields and military hospitals, concluded, "[T]he real war will never get in the books."[11] Symbolic blood is, however, another matter.

D. W. Griffith's film epic *The Birth of a Nation* (1915), his adaptation of *The Clansman* (1905) by Thomas F. Dixon, recognizes the novel as a romance of blood in history and in cultural myth.[12] Griffith understood the strong visceral currents of blood and race in the national narrative of his time, and turned, almost singlehandedly, the narrative of race suicide into the narrative of national (and racial) rebirth. He did it simply, through the overt use of racist stereotypes for full blacks and mulattoes, and with a degree of complexity, through his use of a double courtship-and-marriage plot uniting superior breeding stock from both North and South. Griffith, however, had help in high places.

The president elected in 1912 was the first southerner (Woodrow Wilson was born in Virginia) to occupy the White House since Andrew Johnson, and he brought into office a set of views on the causes and outcomes of the war shaped by his region and by his profession—he was an academic historian not long before he was an elected officeholder. Nothing in Wilson's views put him at odds with the national consensus on the causes and outcomes of the war. Among the causes, for example, slavery and emancipation decidedly did *not* loom large in the Wilsonian view of the Civil War. Emancipation, as a cause for going to war, was a rationale almost wholly determined north of the Mason-Dixon line, for, in Wilson's view, there was little or nothing in slavery itself (not in the practice, not in the psychology of the slaves) that would have pointed to a desire for emancipation.

First, according to Wilson, the slave was fundamentally incapable of and disinclined to favor freedom. Wilson concluded that slaves were too "ignorant" (*Epochs* 120, 125) and too lazy by innate temper (126) to conceive of nonslave life before the War or to grasp the meaning of liberty after the war (261).[13] Lacking any understanding of modernity, black slaves were appropriately placed in lives of controlled agricultural work. Since Wilson concluded that, at the turn of the century, the War and its aftermath (Reconstruction) were "now possible to discuss without passion" (122), it could be stated in public without fear of contradiction or shame that the African population in the South was "too numerous and too ignorant to be safely set free" (125), that "domestic slaves [in the deeper South far away from Border States] were almost uniformly dealt with indulgently and even affectionately by their masters" (125), and that field hands "were comfortably quartered, and were kept from overwork both by their own laziness and by the slack discipline to which they were subjected" (126). "[P]ossible cases of inhuman conduct toward slaves," such as those enshrined in Harriet Beecher Stowe's *Uncle Tom's Cabin* (1852), were isolated and atypical, and usually occurred in border states where abolitionist agitators had more convenient access to the enslaved population. Southern slave owners, Wilson reasoned, kept their human property in chains not because they themselves were morally evil but, rather, because they were rational and humane men who saw that it would be unwise to set "free a body of men so large, so ignorant, and so unskilled in the moderate use of freedom" (120). Slavery did not exist because vast plantations required a large and enslaved workforce; the large enslaved workforce existed because "the slothful and negligent slave" could not learn any skills but the most rudimentary and therefore could be of no use in other, more advanced "modes of farming" (128). In other words, the slave population was an internal and domestic accumulation of human beings that could be described in terms Theodore Roosevelt had used in outlining U.S. imperial adventures around the world: "mere savages," or "a mild and kindly race," or a "people that has not already a high civilization of its own."[14]

In Wilson's view, then, Reconstruction—including the constitutionally mandated emancipation and enfranchisement of the former slaves enforced by an occupying armed force—was a misbegotten federal program destined to call forth the evils so graphically depicted in the southern fiction of his era, notably that of Thomas F. Dixon: unwarranted misery suffered by elite southern whites dispossessed of their wealth, failure of public order in regimes run by and for "the somewhat bewildered and quite helpless hosts of liberated slaves" (263), and interracial sexual threats to the repopulation of the white race. Such narratives were history, not propaganda. Little wonder, then, that limits on the civil rights of the freedmen should be officially legislated (*Plessy v. Ferguson* [1896] standing in for the vast Jim Crow state apparatus) or unofficially exercised by vigilante gangs like the Ku Klux Klan. The end of Reconstruction in 1876 was not, in Wilson's view, the defeat of the better angels of our nature by cynical electoral politics but the appropriate restoration of "the natural, inevitable ascendancy of the whites, the responsible class" (273).

Wilson's historian's narrative is a powerful romance in which European, white civilization triumphs over a rising tide of nonwhite blood and its own self-inflicted slaughter of breeding stock. But the story is not the kind to excite and unify the imagination of a people. Wilson himself consistently evaded confrontation with the actual history of the conflict. Invited to attend the fiftieth anniversary of the Battle of Gettysburg in July 1913, he at first begged off, preferring to vacation in New Hampshire during a particularly hot summer. But he was eventually persuaded to speak and, in a mixture of what David Blight describes as idealism and ambiguity, succeeded in paying tribute to the veterans of both sides in remarks that included only one utterance of the word "race": "How wholesome and healing the peace has been! We have found one another again as brothers and comrades in arms, enemies no longer, generous friends rather, our battles long past, the quarrel forgotten."[15] Not only was the bloody war forgotten, rhetorically downgraded to a quarrel, but the millions of slaves emancipated and then abandoned to continued segregation were forgotten as well; it was a Jim Crow reunion, in Blight's view (9). Elsewhere in *Race and Reunion*, David Blight amply points out the thoroughness with which "blood" saturated the political rhetoric of the time: the "bloody shirt" was flourished by both northern and southern politicians in every election campaign in which there was a respectable number of voters who were veterans; "martyr's blood" was invoked at every battlefield memorial; and the water of baptism (the religious rite of initiation into a special identity) was replaced in oratory, sermon, and editorial with baptism in the blood of the Civil War dead (51–52). Drew Gilpin Faust, in *The Republic of Suffering: Death and the American Civil War* (2008), confirms the thoroughness with which "blood" soaked the rhetoric of politics, pulpit oratory, and private correspondence. By the time of the semicentennial Americans had to reconcile rhetorical blood to the emerging science of blood. In fact, entailing so much rhetoric of blood, and so much more suppressed memory of the liters of actual blood shed on battlefields or spurted and smeared on surgeons' ungloved hands and aprons, Civil War memory after fifty years drew energy (often of the darker kind) from the narrative of blood.[16]

Interweaving Wilson's bloodless romance of national amnesia and reconciliation with the highly charged symbolic blood of the contemporary imagination, D. W. Griffith's *The Birth of a Nation* adapts two melodramatic and racist novels by North Carolinian Thomas F. Dixon and the cooler presentation of Wilson's history into a milestone of filmmaking and racist propaganda.[17] *The Leopard's Spots* (1902), the earlier of the two Dixon novels, is also the cruder of the two. The novel, which begins in 1865 with the fall of the Confederacy, follows the life and career of Charlie Gaston, a North Carolinian whose father, a colonel in the CSA, is killed toward the end of the war. News of the elder Gaston's heroic death is brought back to the homeplace by the family's faithful slave, Nelse. Nelse brings the master's dying wishes that his son be reared "to a glorious manhood in the new nation that will be born in this agony" (13). The shock of losing her husband sends the widow Gaston into hysterical prostration, and eight-year-old Charlie gets an early baptism in the burden of southern memory and in the debt (sexual, psychological, cultural) that the surviving male owes to the grieving women. As a surviving, if immature, breeding male of the superior strain, Charlie must not only triumph in the political plot of redemption from illegitimate occupation and reconstruction by a foreign power (the Union), but also in the romance of reconstructing the procreative white family. Dixon's hero is indebted to his biological mother for being born through her pain, and in his repayment he must continue the birthing of the new nation by finding the right mate to restore, as eugenicist arguments might phrase it, the superior strain put in jeopardy by so many battlefield deaths and by the freeing of so many "inferior" breeding men and women.

Charlie Gaston survives Reconstruction and the wreck of his family with the help of two father surrogates: Rev. John Durham (a transparent stand-in for Dixon himself) who delivers ever more strident and racist diatribes against emancipation and race mixing as *The Leopard's Spots* grinds along, and yeoman Tom Camp, who has the doubly tragic misfortune to lose two daughters to rape by "black beasts." Negotiating extremes of white racism above and below him in class, Charlie matures into the idealized white patrician. In tribute, Nelse, on his deathbed, bequeaths Charlie his banjo, a cultural symbol Dixon must have known to be heavily loaded with African American meaning. Dixon's laudable African Americans, like the inferior civilizations Roosevelt saw as inevitable beneficiaries of "American or European ideas," acknowledge that they are not the best custodians of their own culture. All others are rapists.

The romance of blood, however, needs a complication, the threat of pollution by the agents of impurity and reversion. Charlie Gaston, the pure Anglo-Saxon hero, must find a mate; the purity of his own blood is one thing but carrying it into the future is another. Beyond romance there is the birth rate to consider. As he struggles to grasp political control, Gaston also has to secure the future of the blood by marrying the appropriate wife. Dixon does some pretty obvious and even deplorable things in the process of eliminating the ineligible mates for the hero. The yeoman Camp's elder daughter, Annie, is taken out of the picture by being shot through the temple after a uniformed squad of freedmen break into her wedding and threaten to rape her. Her father exclaims that "[t]here are things worse than death!" and begs his white friends to shoot her—they oblige (125). Years later another young daughter is raped and killed by another renegade black man. Other female characters who might occupy parts of the scheme are similarly tainted. A white woman from Boston, who finances and teaches in a school for the freedmen, is condemned by Rev. Durham as a "feminine bulldog" (45). Dixon reserves a fate worse than celibacy for her much later in The Leopard's Spots when he marries her to Simon Legree, Stowe's archvillain, whom Dixon kidnaps into his novel and eventually transports to a lucrative position on Wall Street.

Charlie ultimately meets his destined mate in Sallie Worth, a beautiful and spirited daughter of a Confederate general who lives in the stereotypical porticoed mansion. There is a rival for Sallie's hand, of course, McLeod, a boyhood pal of Charlie's who has gone over to the dark side by enlisting in the Republican Reconstruction government, the integrated regime Charlie is fated to "redeem." Redemption comes about, as it did in history when southern whites successfully disenfranchised black men at the close of Reconstruction, when Charlie and Sallie are married in the governor's mansion at the end of the novel. A nuptial rite enacted in a site of government functions as an overt fusing of political and romantic wish fulfillment.

But before the predictable ending in the marriage of two racially pure, white lovers, a scene redundant to the propagandistic purpose of the novel occurs: the rape of Tom Camp's second daughter. Camp, the yeoman who had given the order to execute his elder daughter on her wedding day, has, we are belatedly informed, fathered a second daughter with his grieving wife who died not long after giving birth. Camp is alone in the world with Flora, a child obviously copied from Stowe's Eva. Flora is the curly blonde embodiment of Anglo-Saxon innocence. She is kind to all and sundry, and fatally kind (as Dixon would have it) to "vagrant" black men who wander the village streets in drunken and benighted freedom. One of these freedmen, Dick, Charlie Gaston's childhood acquisition as a playmate and evil double, rapes Flora and bashes her blonde head with a stone, bringing forth the blood so deeply resonant in the wider cultural narrative. A transfusion apparatus makes a momentary appearance in the text when Charlie Gaston volunteers to donate his own blood to save the mortally injured Flora (374), but she dies before donor and recipient can be connected.

Camp and the rest of the white men of the town metamorphose into a Ku Klux Klan posse and apprehend Dick. Dick pleads with Gaston for rescue on the basis of their history as lifelong master and servant, and Gaston in turn begs the Klan for a trial. His plea is rejected and Dick is incinerated (377). By inserting a second rape event, Dixon enflames the racial theme of *The Leopard's Spots* repeatedly stated in the text by his surrogate, Durham, in one speech after another. By adding the failed transfusion, Dixon pushes readers to think of blood both historically and symbolically. The raped Flora (like Lucy Westenra punctured and drained by Dracula) looms as a specter of the white female body polluted by black blood through a sexual act and resonates as all the more evocative because that act could be vividly imagined yet could not be named. In both literary cases, *Dracula* and *The Leopard's Spots,* the preliminary cure for blood pollution is to fight bad blood with pure. In neither case does the cure succeed; such is the popular anxiety about the "rising tide of color." The inundation of whiteness with pollution becomes a significant element of the Civil War plot just as scientific research began to conclude that blood types might be different but not because of the race of the donor.[18]

Once mixed, pure symbolic blood cannot be purified again, so the emphasis on preserving purity must be the first priority of romantic plots and subplots. In yet another superfluous subplot in *The Leopard's Spots,* Dixon imports Stowe's George Harris, the brilliant but violence-prone mulatto of *Uncle Tom's Cabin,* and gives him a Bostonian education and a fatal attraction to Helen Lowell, the daughter of his northern benefactor. When Harris, confronting Mr. Lowell with the white man's own pledges of racial equality, asks for permission to court Helen, the white father becomes adamant:

> "Nevertheless, [Lowell tells Harris] you are a negro and I do not desire the infusion of your blood in my family."
> "But I have more of white than negro blood."
> "So much the worse. It is a mark of shame." (391)

Pathbreaking blood science at the turn of the century was beginning to suggest that blood is blood and that transfusion might soon become a common procedure. But several times in *The Leopard's Spots,* Dixon places pure white blood in jeopardy, sexualized in the courtship and marriage plots, and brings these images to the reader's attention, adding anxiety about "infusion" to the spreading scientific fact of transfusion. In the subplot involving George Harris and his potential white patrician father-in-law, the threat of "reversion" (the mathematically and culturally certain return of the repressed impure blood flagged by Galton) surfaces as a fatal barrier to courtship. Harris might argue that he possesses a higher percentage of white blood than black, but the master race (in this scene, the Bostonian Lowell) can live only with certainties, never with probabilities, and so George Harris is dismissed as a certain, if future, cause of pollution.

About the time *The Birth of a Nation* stirred up Anglo-Saxon race and blood hysteria in 1915, yet another manifestation of the trope of race-infused blood drove the public mind to defensive positions. Edward Sheldon's *"The Nigger": An American Play in Three Acts* opened and closed on Broadway in December 1909, but it was reissued by Macmillan in 1915 following its adaptation to film that year.[19] In some of the reports of NAACP field offices detailing their protests against Griffith's film, local activists include protests against the screening of *The Governor* (1915)—the less incendiary title of the film made from Sheldon's play. They were wholly successful in neither case.

Rather than close with a rape and lynching, which was Dixon's preferred plot arc, Sheldon's play opens with the rape of a white woman by a black man. The rapist, a black man named Joe, flees to the columned southern mansion of Phil Morrow (respected local sheriff and soon-to-be governor) hoping for protection. He has reason to think he might find sanctuary in Morrow's house, and his mother, Mammy Jinny of familiar stereotype, knows a secret that might bolster the fugitive's hope. For two acts the plot runs on the familiar octane of white romance and political rivalry (over prohibition of liquor, not the typical issue of Reconstruction politics). The climax dawns, however, not when Phil Morrow's fiancée Georgie Byrd wrestles with the discovery that she is the tragic mulatto, her blood "infused" with racial impurity, but when Phil himself finds out—from Mammy Jinny—that he is his white father's son by a mulatto woman, switched at birth after the master's "pure" white son died—a trope central to Mark Twain's *Pudd'nhead Wilson* (1894). The revelation that he is not pure white is all the more intense since Phil Morrow, because of his prohibitionist policies, is portrayed as a progressive politician in the antebellum South, albeit a "progressive" who still believes "'[t]hings have changed some since the wah, an' if we want t' keep our blood clean, we've got to know that *white's white* an' *black's black*—an' mixin' 'em's damnation'" (33). One can easily imagine this, in 1909 and in 1915, as a fail-safe applause line with a white audience.

In a plot twist daring for its time, the hero, recently elected governor of his southern state, opts to live with his new and surprising cross-racial identity. Not only does he reject the Dixonian tenet (and his own earlier statement) that nothing is worse than racial mixing, but his fiancée does as well. Georgie first accepts their broken engagement, then returns to the governor's mansion in the final scene to stand by her man as he exits the stage ready to tell an assembled crowd the story of his real identity. This represents a breakthrough for Georgie as well, for in an earlier scene when she learns of the lynching of Joe, she reacts by saying, "'[A]fter all . . . well, he's only a negro'" (Sheldon 100). In a few lines of dialogue that have to rank as some of the most eerily prophetic in American literary history, one of the new governor's black political advisors tells Phil that "a hundred yeahs from now" (1908–09 to 2008–09) he, newly aware of his mixed-race identity, will look foolish for allowing it to disqualify him from serving in public office (210).

The blood romance that shaped the American mind in the era

of the fiftieth anniversary of the Civil War was very seldom as daring and exploratory as Sheldon's *The Governor*. Thomas F. Dixon's follow-up to *The Leopard's Spots* is *The Clansman* (1905), the story most fully adapted into *The Birth of a Nation*. In *The Clansman*, one of a series of historical novels "on the Race Conflict" Dixon planned, the "romance" is doubled intentionally (1). Ben Cameron, a handsome southern man, courts Elsie Stoneman, the daughter of a Quaker mother and a Puritan father, and her brother, Phil, in turn courts and marries Ben Cameron's sister, Margaret. The romance of national reunion and rebirth is covered in multiple variations of bloodlines: the Puritan, the Quaker, and—in the Cameron siblings—the heroic "Scotch Covenanter blood" under threat of extinction first in the Civil War and then by Reconstruction (100). We may read Dixon's plot contortions as a direct response to fears of "race suicide." Indeed, when Griffith's film was initially released in 1915, it bore Dixon's title, *The Clansman*. To deflect opposition by the newly organized NAACP and local boards of censorship, Griffith, at Dixon's urging, changed the title to *The Birth of a Nation*. Public censors in Boston and other cities and towns demanded the cutting of some scenes (usually the rape scene) lest a showing of the unedited film lead to civil disorder.[20] Led by W. E. B. Du Bois, the NAACP, founded in 1909, made revocation of permission to show *The Birth of a Nation* the focus of national and local chapter campaigns all through 1915. Their success was uneven. Some jurisdictions insisted on edits, which were often never completed. In one very influential venue, the film was shown uncensored: Woodrow Wilson's White House.

The NAACP's objections to Griffith's film were ignited by the stark and bigoted caricatures of racial types both Dixon and Griffith used in their storytelling.[21] Dixon and Griffith broke the hush of academic manners (as practiced by Wilson and others) by thrusting images of sex and blood to the foreground of the story. The sex and blood of the romance plot in *The Leopard's Spots* is akin to the sex and blood in *The Clansman / The Birth of a Nation*. When Dixon uses mulatto characters (Lydia Brown, Austin Stoneman's housekeeper and perhaps his mistress; Silas Lynch, the mulatto man he grooms to run the Reconstruction regime in Piedmont, Dixon's semifictional southern town), he charges them with sexual "un-discipline"—that is, they are propelled by a blood that cannot be tamed. Lydia Brown's first appearance in the novel is a clear example: "No more curious or sinister figure ever cast a shadow across the history of a great nation than did this mulatto woman in the most corrupt hour of American life. The grim old man [Stoneman] who looked into her sleek tawny face and followed her catlike eyes was steadily gripping the Nation by the throat. Did he aim to make this woman the arbiter of its social life, and her ethics the limit of its moral laws?" (94). In a later scene, Dixon labels Lydia Brown, and all mulatto women, as symbols of a civic "gangrene" (156). Choosing a metaphor from the range of blood diseases is not wholly accidental in Dixon's time, awash as it was with infusions and transfusions of blood. Lydia Brown's white patron, Austin Stoneman may be unable to resist her heat, but Silas Lynch, her ironically named mulatto counterpart in the plot, operates as her coconspirator. As they pass in the corridor outside Stoneman's chamber, Dixon writes that "a close observer might have seen him [Silas Lynch] suddenly press her [Lydia Brown's] hand and [catch] her sly answering smile" (94). The mixed-race couple has sealed a sexual alliance to manipulate their white sponsor; the mixed blood beyond white purity is predictable in only one characteristic—it is always intent on becoming, or usurping, the white.

Griffith's segregationist casting policy—each of the featured black or mulatto characters in *The Birth of a Nation* is played by a white actor in blackface—directly embodies the racist doctrine voiced in Dixon's text. Dixon signals Lynch's danger to white blood purity in his written description: "On his [Stone-man's] left sat a negro of perhaps forty years, a man of charm-ing features for a mulatto, who had evidently inherited the full physical characteristics of the Aryan race, while his dark yellow-ish eyes beneath his heavy brows glowed with the brightness of the African jungle" (93). The sometimes paranoid romance of blood is clearly indicated in the juxtaposition of "Aryan," car-rying the connotations of civilization and progress, which have subsequently been compromised, and the counter-suggestions of sexual power in Lynch's "dark yellowish eyes . . . finely chis-eled lips . . . [and] broad shoulders" (93). That power is physi-cally and thematically realized in a later scene in which Lynch, amid the tumult of a race war, forcefully proposes marriage to Elsie, Stoneman's daughter, who struggles against him but faints in his arms. Elsie Stoneman is not raped by Silas Lynch, although by the racist rules of the time his manhandling of her physically would have amounted to the same thing. Surviving footage of rehearsals for this scene suggests that Griffith worked on it at least as much as he did on his large battle scenes.

Nevertheless, there is a rape in *The Clansman*, and both Dixon and Griffith make it the tightly wound knot of their shared narrative, calling on the white public's obsession with blood and sex to seal their acceptance of the story. Marion Lenoir and her mother, impoverished neighbors of the Cam-erons, who function as the central southern family of the story, are raped by a "semi-barbaric" freed black, Gus, whose libidi-nous desires have been politically liberated by the occupying regime.[22] The victims, returning to consciousness after their or-deal, face the cultural "fact" that they have been fatally pol-luted and, in shame, commit suicide together by leaping over a cliff. Some of Marion's blood, collected from the site of her death, becomes crucial to the Klan ritual that incites the local white males to vigilante violence. They need little urging, espe-cially Ben Cameron, the local (undercover) Grand Dragon of the KKK, who justifies the Klan's existence when he tells his father, who is reluctant to support the vigilantes, that after political and social equality for the freedmen, the raping of white women is the next step (262).

To give the lynching of Gus a religious echo, Ben sifts the sand at the spot of Marion's death for a ceremonial cup of blood-soaked grains. In an imitation of the sacrament of transubstantiation, the cup is filled with water and the bloody sand turned back into the living blood of Marion Lenoir (324). Then the Grand Dragon, Ben Cameron—romantic lover and historical avenger—quenches a fiery cross "in the sweetest blood that ever stained the sands of Time" (326). The assembled Klansmen weep with fury, then perform the bloody murder of Gus and reinstate white supremacy in a campaign of terror. Memories of a civil war and a house divided rapidly disappear. Phil Stoneman, former Union officer, begs to be allowed to ride with the Klan; the imperative of race identity supplants the actual causes and results of the war. The freed slaves, whose emancipation was the highest goal of the Civil War, are transformed into its conquered, reenslaved victims. Griffith turned Dixon's ending into a full-blown race war and tacked a mysterious allegorical dream sequence to the close of the film that Aryanizes Jesus Christ and the redeemed in heaven. Griffith makes sure to emphasize that the Blood of the Lamb is definitely white.

Blood is the common denominator of romance and history in the era of the fiftieth anniversary of the Civil War—blood was *what* the white public chose to remember and the *how* of remembering it. Dixon and Griffith, as crude as their use of stereotype might have been, sensed that compelling fact of storytelling: they could boost the message of fear of race suicide with an image that could work on metaphorical and literal levels simultaneously. The image of white American blood brought remembrance of the Civil War into the present in much more immediate ways than, for example, Woodrow Wilson's genteel prose. As forcefully as historians and eugenicists and sociologists might have invoked blood-in-history as an irrepressible fact of identity—national, tribal, racial—their arguments lacked the emotional thrust to escape rational gravitational fields and connect with a wide, diverse public on a visceral level. But blood-in-romance, sexualized in the raped bodies of white women, nationalized in the sanctioned marriage of white hero and heroine, first inflamed white audiences against African Americans, then quelled passions with images of perpetuated racial mastery running, as Griffith fantasized, from now until eternity, from earth to heaven.

CHAPTER TWO

The Last Living Memory

Over fifty-three thousand veterans of the Civil War registered to attend the fiftieth anniversary of the Battle of Gettysburg in July 1913. Twenty-five years later, in 1938 at the seventy-fifth reunion of the armies who fought at Gettsyburg, approximately 2,000 of the 8,000 to 10,000 living Civil War veterans attended the event (each one furnished with an attendant at federal expense). The ratio at Gettysburg in 1938 was three Union veterans for every Confederate. The anonymous writer for United Press solemnly noted that this would be the vets' "last reunion."[1] He was right. Eighteen years later, on August 2, 1956, Albert Woolson, the last member in good standing of the ever-dwindling cohort of Civil War vets, died in Duluth, Minnesota. He had been born in Antwerp, a town in upstate New York, in 1847. When his father was wounded in the Battle of Shiloh in April 1862, and transported to a hospital in Minnesota (where he later died of his wounds), Woolson's mother traveled with her teenaged son from New York to Minnesota to care for her husband. There was no professional nursing corps during the Civil War. Clara Barton had organized some volunteers in the eastern theater of the war in 1861, but the founding of the American Red Cross was two decades in the future.

After his father died, Albert enlisted as a drummer boy in the First Minnesota Heavy Artillery. When he died in 1956, he was the last surviving member of the Grand Army of the Republic, and the last verifiable veteran of the Civil War on either side. The last genuine Confederate veteran, Pleasant Crump (1847–1951), had died in 1951. Three pretenders to the title "last surviving Civil War veteran" (all claiming to be Confederate soldiers) lived on in the 1950s, but their claims had been debunked while they lived or soon after their deaths.[2] Woolson's picture made it to the front page of several newspapers across the country, including the *St. Petersburg Times*, which also ran a boilerplate statement from President Eisenhower: "His passing brings sorrow to the hearts of all of us who cherished the memory of the brave men on both sides of the War Between the States."[3] Members of the Minnesota National Guard stood watch over the veteran's body at the mortuary, and an honor guard of 109 Guard members (one for each year of Woolson's long life) lined the entrance to the cemetery. Ten Starfire fighter jets flew over the rites in the formation of a cross, and young boys (some in Cub Scout uniforms) held toy rifles at "present arms" as the funeral procession rolled down their leafy streets.

Life Magazine dispatched a crew to Duluth to witness Woolson's funeral and to photograph the event for the nation, and Bruce Catton was commissioned to explain the meaning bound up in Woolson's life and death. Catton's name was already attached to several books about the Civil War, and in a few years he would become the authority on its centennial history. David W. Blight, in *American Oracle,* writes that Catton became "a household brand name for Civil War enthusiasm" and later, during the one hundredth anniversary, for "Centennial fatigue."[4] Catton's ruminations on Woolson's death are, curiously, neither enthusiastic nor fatigued. His tone is deeply mournful, broadening the vague sorrow for "the last reunion" voiced by the commentator on the seventy-fifth Gettysburg reunion. Catton's obituary for one man reads like an obituary for an era and suggests that the coming centennial might be more funereal than celebratory. Beginning with the announcement that "something deeply and fundamentally American is gone forever" (19), Catton concludes with "we have lost something we can never regain" (23).[5] He was not the only centennial watcher who worried that legitimate remembrance might drift out of reach with the passing of living links to the past. Robert Penn Warren fretted that "family pieties . . . thin . . . with time" and that "few men now alive can, chronologically, have known the grandfather who had been in the War."[6] Warren's maternal grandfather Gabriel Penn (1836–1920) had been such a chronological link.

The longing, nostalgic backward look shared by Catton and Warren and stretching across the century seems all the more significant as prologue to the centennial when we remember that the public turmoil of the civil rights movement, waxing rather than waning, coincided with the centennial of the Civil War. Losing the last living link to the great national epic of the Civil War seemed to Catton to mean a loss of direction in memorialization. The centennial loomed—just five years off in 1956—and Catton's musings on the meaning of Woolson's life and death crept very gingerly toward the great anxiety that, with no focal point in the past, public attention might inevitably be swallowed by the present. The present that daily pressured the American public in the 1950s and lay in wait for the centennial was the movement for civil rights. In 1956 the Montgomery bus boycott was underway, and the admission of Autherine Lucy to the University of Alabama caused white riots in Tuscaloosa. Despite these events, Catton attempts to position the Civil War in the present of Woolson's death without overtly naming the great irresistible force shaping that present: "By fighting the Civil War the nation had unconsciously dedicated itself to two lofty, almost unattainable goals: to the no-tion that there must be a unity in human society—that no man is finally an island, that we are members of one another, that our salvation must eventually lie in the striving toward brotherhood—and to the idea that human freedom is something that goes all across the board" (21–22). "That dual goal," Catton continues, "will not be reached for a very long time, but the effort to reach it is what gives American life its deepest significance" (22). In the summer of 1956, such language would have been heard by many Americans as little more than pious obfuscation. The blatant substitution of "striving toward" for "brotherhood" itself was often the evasive retreat of the white liberal. Moreover, to describe the objectives of the Thirteenth, Fourteenth, and Fifteenth Amendments to the Constitution (abolishing slavery, establishing citizenship, and insuring the suffrage) as "unconscious" amounts as well to an evasive misreading of their entwined purposes. Catton's sermonic rhetoric about the loss of the past only serves to sidestep direct confrontation with the fact that the nation had failed to deliver on the clear promises made after the Civil War to free those who had been enslaved and to admit them to full citizenship. That those promises would remain unfulfilled "for a very long time" is, yet again, the familiar claim by those who hold power that justice delayed is, somehow, still justice.[7]

With the portentous passing of the last veteran of the Civil War and the approaching centennial, pressure to make good on promises made to the freedmen and -women of that war came not only from within the country but also from foreign antagonists eager to see the United States fail. The centennial, Catton and others knew, would be celebrated in the anxious atmosphere of the Cold War. Only a few months after the burial of Albert Woolson, the people of Hungary would try to liberate themselves from Soviet rule—and be forcefully drawn back. In such a world, Catton recognized, the United States must present itself as a "bulwark against a rising tide of dictatorship and oppression" (23). That bulwark would be mocked as a Potemkin façade if the meaning of the Civil War were steered toward costume and pageantry redolent of the past and away from the very real and very present politics of civil rights. But pageantry, as the Minnesota funeral of Albert Woolson illustrated, was likely the more comfortable of the two options.

Civil War pageantry, as Catton and others were learning as the centennial advanced, had a limited shelf life. In April 1961, the annual meeting of the Civil War Centennial Commission, established by Congress in 1957 to coordinate plans for a national observation, was disrupted when the conference hotel in Charleston, South Carolina, refused to provide accommodations to African American members of the delegation from New Jersey. Eventually the meeting was moved to the Charleston Navy Yard, a federal facility and therefore officially desegregated. But the damage had been done to the image of the centennial as a festival and to the nostalgia-themed intentions of many of the leaders of the commission. In the summer of 1961, a heavily promoted reenactment of the First Battle of Bull Run, organized by the National Park Service with the aid of commercial sponsorships, was a fiasco. By late summer, the honorary chairman of the commission, U. S. Grant III (the former president's grandson) had resigned.[8] Scarcely a year into the centennial, the fissures were widening.

The waning power of the Civil War to ignite public interest could also be seen in the pale reenactment of the premiere of *Gone with the Wind* that took place in Atlanta in March 1961. In December 1939, between the Great Depression and the onset of the Second World War, the original premiere of the film was a ritual of southern tribalism and regional pride far in excess of material facts. "After all," David O. Selznick wrote to Kay Brown, who was in charge of arrangements in Atlanta in 1939, "we have only made a motion picture."[9] Organizers of the premiere in Atlanta saw it as much more than a motion picture. Selznick might have had reason to be skeptical of premiere fever. His studio was in shaky financial condition. Money from ticket sales to *Gone with the Wind* and *Rebecca* (1940), another Selznick film adapted from a best-selling novel, had yet to flow in. Clark Gable had to be prodded to come to Atlanta; Vivien Leigh, miffed that she had not been cast opposite her husband Laurence Olivier in *Rebecca*, was bridling that MGM had asked "her to go to a provincial town, for hicks, and wear Scarlett's costumes" (Thomson 321). Organizers in Atlanta, over Selznick's objections, nixed African American Hattie McDaniel's photo from the souvenir program, and the actress herself was persuaded not to attend (322). Still, Margaret Mitchell, in remarks broadcast over radio, spoke for an entire (white) region when she said: "I feel like it's been a very great thing for Georgia and the South to see our old Confederacy come back to us" (324). Acts and rituals of collective memory have strange and often tenuous relationships to actual circumstances, and for communities of believers (here: "Georgia and the South") the material circumstances ("only . . . a motion picture") are invisible as the past "come[s] back to us," reestablishing the "us" in a historical rush always moving away from its last living presence.

Reinvoking the past in the present teems with cultural risk because the reach of the present into the past is everyday more distant, and what seems authentic about the past might seem fraudulent in the present. Lightning never striking twice is not the only cliché that applies to 1961. When promoters in Atlanta attempted the "re-premiere" in 1961, they faced serious obstacles. Mitchell had died in 1949, Hattie McDaniel in 1952, and Clark Gable in 1960. Selznick himself was seriously ill and no longer owned the rights to *Gone with the Wind*.[10] Vivien Leigh, looking fragile and worn, and Olivia deHavilland, appearing unchanged, attended the re-premiere, but Hollywood magic did not revisit the centennial. Expectations of large profits to fund other events in Georgia's centennial celebration did not materialize.[11]

Reenactment as a fool's errand, rather than legitimate memory, was the verdict of Flannery O'Connor, who dissected the Civil War with her customary desert-dry irony in "A Late Encounter with the Enemy," a short story about a Civil War impostor, which was written in 1953 (when the three Civil War veteran impostors noted earlier, all southerners, were still alive) and published a couple of years later (1955) in *Harper's Bazaar*. Confederate general "Tennessee" Flintrock Sash embodies the porous barrier between Civil War memory and cultural delusion, a reenactor before the trend became so popular.[12] Compelled to attend his granddaughter's graduation after her laborious and extended career in college (twenty years of summer school), the general slips into a netherworld of confusion where he recalls attending the 1939 premiere of the film *Gone with the Wind* in Atlanta, which seems to be the only event even approximating Civil War service he has actually known. He is convinced of one thing, though: "When he put on his full dress general's uniform, he knew well enough there was nothing to match him anywhere."[13] Not even his younger self could match the image in his fantasy, for O'Connor tells us the old man had never been a general and had probably never worn a Confederate uniform of any rank. She must have taken wry pleasure several years after her story's publication to see in a 1959 issue of *Life* magazine a short feature about Walter Williams, a supposed Confederate general, which included a photograph of him lounging in bed smoking a cigar, a braided Confederate officer's uniform hanging alongside U.S. and CSA flags serving as his headboard and shrine. The artist Larry Rivers used the photograph as the model for his painting "The Last Civil War Veteran" (1961). Williams was later proven to be an impostor.[14]

Sally Poker Sash, the ersatz general's granddaughter, is grimly determined that the old man survive just long enough to be wheeled onto the stage as she is handed her diploma. She is brewing up sweet revenge: "See him! See him! My kin, all you upstarts! Glorious upright old man standing for the old traditions! Duty! Honor! Courage!" (135). The irony is that the old man cannot physically stand (he has lost feeling in his legs and feet), and does not symbolically stand for anything except the "tradition" of "parades with floats full of Miss Americas and Miss Daytona Beaches and Miss Queen Cotton Products" (134). Sally has arranged for her nephew, Boy Scout John Wesley Poker Sash, to roll the general to the stage in a wheelchair. But the boy, "a fat blond boy with an executive expression" (140), keeps detouring to the Coca-Cola machine—a new tradition in the South making millionaires of not a few upstarts. Before Sally receives her diploma, the general dies, expiring in a fugue of Civil War names and places. In O'Connor's story, unlike Catton's eulogy, the loss of a link to the past is unlamented since said link was never much more than a mummy, "bundled up and lent to the Capitol City Museum [each Confederate Memorial Day] where he was displayed from one to four in a musty room full of old photographs, old uniforms, old artillery, and historic documents" (139). In the final scene of the story, O'Connor poses a striking tableau: a dead fake general in line to a Coca-Cola machine with a Boy Scout who has no idea he is waiting with a corpse for the "pause that refreshes." One Old South artifact (of doubtful authenticity) dead, a New South consumer economy working just fine, and the next generation oblivious to its past. Welcome to the centennial.

Flannery O'Connor was not impressed with southern pieties; indeed, given her deep theological commitments, the past that concerned her stretched well beyond the 1860s. Nor was the South her religion: "I sure am sick of the Civil War" is not a mantra that motivates reunions or encampments.[15] Nevertheless, O'Connor's story suggests the complicated politics of

Civil War memory in the era of civil rights. The Boy Scout at the Coca-Cola machine will soon enter the orbit of the Civil War centennial. Somewhere between the vending machine and the dead general, he will be officially asked to find a future in his past. "Each time a tradition is articulated," historian Fitzhugh Brundage writes, "it must be given a meaning appropriate to the historical context in which it is invoked. For a historical memory to retain its capacity to speak and mobilize its intended audience, it must address contemporary concerns about the past" (9–10). At the fiftieth anniversary, when tens of thousands of the veterans of both sides of the Civil War were still alive and World War I had not yet revised our Homeric definition of warfare, the community of historical memory was comparatively more united than it would ever be again. Commemoration registered as more vividly present than a reenactment. As the centennial bore down upon 1961, however, there were no living connections to the Civil War, and into that void seeped a great anxiety that (with an active civil rights movement compelling direct political attention in the present) cozy, nostalgic reaffirmations of comradeship under northern and southern arms, the theme of Eisenhower's banal comment on the death of Albert Woolson, might have become dangerously shopworn.

Unlike Flannery O'Connor, who diagnosed Civil War fatigue before the centennial, many commentators looked upon the one hundredth anniversary with a range of lively feelings. A writer for the left-leaning *Nation*, L. Jesse Lemisch, took a characteristic (for him) radical approach: "How did this come about? How did it happen that for the next four years we will be celebrating an unprecedented event—a war without villains? In large part, this perverse festival has its origins in the psychic needs of a people who fought for what they know to be a shameful cause—and lost."[16] The not-so-subtle slip in verb tense (know/knew) signals the ongoing presence of the Civil

War in the emergent radical atmosphere of the early 1960s and reflects the anxiety that the South might yet win the battle for the hearts and minds of Americans: "The official commemoration of the Civil War constitutes a surrender to the South" (Lemisch 302).[17]

Edmund Wilson thought the official centennial less "perverse" than "absurd."[18] Judging solely by the title of his study of the literature of the Civil War, *Patriotic Gore* (1962), you might think the power of the blood metaphor had survived. But Wilson was no connoisseur of heroes or tragedy. The fifty years between 1911 and 1961 had produced a United States that, in Wilson's estimation, could no longer think of war and heroism in the same moment of public memory. A nation for whom the triumph of the Second World War had wasted into the ambiguous surrogate games of the Cold War had learned a distinctly antiheroic lesson, according to Wilson, but would probably fail to recognize it.

Maybe Wilson had been breathing the Cold War air when he wrote not of blood but of an image much colder and slimier: "Now, the wars fought by human beings are stimulated as a rule by the same instincts as the voracity of the sea slug" (xi). In Wilson's jaundiced view, the sea slug represented the blind appetite for power. Like the sea slug, he wrote, the North crushed the South simply because it could. Abolition of slavery was merely a "rabble-rousing issue which [was] necessary . . . to make the conflict appear as a melodrama" and thereby motivate an otherwise apathetic public to commit mayhem against fellow citizens (xvi). "The North's determination to preserve the Union," Wilson concluded, "was simply the form that the power drive now took" (xvi). The emerging trinity of the civil religion of civil rights (Abraham, Martin, and John) was, in Wilson's world-weary view, actually a melodramatic front for a troika of power-hungry nation builders: Lincoln, Bismarck, and Lenin.[19]

Wilson saw his *Patriotic Gore* as an attempt "to remove the whole subject [of the Civil War] from the plane of morality and to give an objective account of the expansion of the United States" (xxxi). Wilson also thought that Robert Penn Warren in his *The Legacy of the Civil War*, published a year before *Patriotic Gore*, had written "the most intelligent comment . . . that has yet been brought forth by this absurd centennial—a day of mourning would be more appropriate" (xxxi). Wilson's praise was based on his assumption that Warren stood with him on a platform charging both northern and southern traditions, insofar as each claimed moral high ground, as "fraudulent" (Wilson xxxi). But Wilson's assumptions were wrong; Warren was not sick of the Civil War, and he did not think the project of remembering it either absurd or perverse. For Warren, the Civil War was far from being a fraud, and the centennial offered a late and possibly final chance to connect to its public meaning.

By 1961 Robert Penn Warren had already made the "legacy of the civil war" a central element in his lifelong interrogation of southern identity. More forthright than Bruce Catton about the part played by race in American identity, Warren was willing to discuss race issues as they shaped both the past and the present. Less jaded than Wilson on the potency of the American presence in history, Warren refused to see the centennial as "absurd." More moderate than Lemisch, he was inclined to be pragmatic, to spread venality across both regions. Themes of race and history run through his work like a motif in a Romantic symphony, shaping his essay in the Agrarian manifesto *I'll Take My Stand*, "The Briar Patch," (1930); his books *John Brown: The Making of a Martyr* (1929); *Segregation: The Inner Conflict in the South* (1956); the quest narrative *Who Speaks for the Negro?* (1965); his book-length essay *The Legacy of the Civil War* (1961); and his novel *Wilderness: A Tale of the Civil War* (1961). The latter two, Warren's purpose-driven attempts to assess the meaning of the Civil War in the present provided by the centennial, should be seen as part of the continuum in his lifelong work to reconcile North and South to the United States and himself to his country. Warren understood the churning of the past in the present, but he habitually insisted that we are obliged to make more meaning than the sea slug. In his most famous novel, *All the King's Men* (1949), his protagonist Jack Burden tries to escape responsibility for history in the near term of his dirty work for Willie Stark and in the long term of History by driving almost nonstop across country. He drives himself psychologically into a deep, almost completely desensitized, stupor. In his altered state Jack theorizes "The Big Twitch," which functions as his way out of responsibility for history and History: human beings act in history the way involuntary tics act in individual organisms, randomly firing neural shots of energy without aim or intention. This is Warren's version of the sea slug, but he discards this view by the end of *All the King's Men*. We are responsible in history and for History; this is what Edmund Wilson failed to see about Warren.

The Legacy of the Civil War began as "A Mark Deep on a Nation's Soul," an article-length feature in the 1961 St. Patrick's Day issue of *Life*. Warren's article was the sixth and final installment in a *Life* series on the centennial of the Civil War, wrapped up in time for the centennial of the bombarding of Fort Sumter.[20] It was in time too, as its contemporary readers knew and we should also remember, to be filed under the heading of the South where Hamilton Holmes and Charlayne Hunter's admission to the University of Georgia (like Autherine Lucy's to the University of Alabama in 1956 and James Meredith's to the University of Mississippi in 1962) caused riots and where in the summer of 1961 Freedom Riders would be jailed in Jackson, Mississippi. The American public—distanced by a century from the historical events of the Civil War—was stretched between imagining the South as an epic battlefield (our "Homeric period," as Warren would call it) and seeing it (often nightly on the news) as a dysfunctional region where battles took place in more mundane venues such as lunch counters, school campuses, and bus stations.

Warren opens both versions of *The Legacy of the Civil War* on the same resonant note of confidence in national consensus about the unity of American identity. Warren, like many of his contemporaries, was not a multiculturalist; indeed, the term had not yet come into fashion. There was for Warren only one America: "The Civil War is for the American imagination the great single event of our history. Without too much wrenching, it may, in fact, be said to *be* American history. Before the Civil War we had no history in the deepest and most inward sense" (RH 3). In an age Warren and his readers well knew to be as divisive and violent as any in peacetime (and primed to become even more deeply split as civil rights activism spread and the war in Southeast Asia emerged from the back pages into the headlines), he felt no qualms about using the collective pronouns of national consensus or possessing the meaning of "American history" in a single phrase. Warren had no reservations about dismissing the Revolution and our founding constitutional deliberations as what he would later in *The Legacy* call "romantic unionism" and, in both versions, devalue as a nation created "on paper" and "merely a daydream of easy and automatic victories, a vulgar delusion of Manifest Destiny, a conviction of being a people divinely chosen to live on milk and honey, at small expense" (L 82; RH 3).

Warren's skepticism of the Founders is quickly asserted: "The vision [of the Founders] had not been finally submitted to the test of history. There was little awareness of the cost of having a history. The anguished scrutiny of the meaning of the vision in experience had not become a national reality" (RH 3–4). The vocabulary of "test" and "cost" and "anguish" transforms the Civil War, as it runs through Warren's imagination, from a historical pageant conducted "out there" in history or in a contemporary ritual into a traumatic, "most inward" event in a national psychodrama. A nation cannot simply be thought into existence with resonant documents like the Declaration of Independence, the Constitution, or the Federalist Papers; a nation has to be suffered into being by the shedding of blood. The "vision" must be submitted to "experience." What Warren feared most at the centennial was that the results of the "test" suffered through one hundred years earlier would be misunderstood by the shallower Americans of the present, that they might miss "the tragic aura of the event" (L 88) because they lacked living witnesses to connect them to it. Warren feared that the necessary inner turmoil of Americans might be smothered by thick layers of complacency, something the 1950s supposedly had in abundance.

The years leading up to the Civil War centennial were fertile soil for such a crisis in public memory. As the official organizers of the public ceremonies (the Civil War Centennial Commission) soon learned, there was no longer a simplistic Civil War narrative with heroic American warriors on both sides. Such a view numbed public memory with cultural amnesia and obscured complex events with formulaic pseudo-understandings. Neither side, Warren insisted, was either perfectly virtuous or irredeemably evil. Without a starting point in worldly complexity (L 82), he argued, no commemoration of the Civil War would be worth a serious public's time and effort. The nation Warren hoped for as the Civil War inevitably receded into the past would be neither a population of battlefield tourists nor competing teams of regional true believers. He aimed for "a true community, a spiritually significant communion" that "the old romantic unionism" of 1776 never could have achieved (RH 6).

Warren's strategy for remembering the Civil War one hundred years after the fact was to replace simplistic gunsmoke-and-bugle narratives with more complex analogies, allegories, and images. In *The Legacy of the Civil War* he opened by dividing the event into Mind and Body. As an event in the evolution of the American Mind, the war of 1861–65 resolved the conflict Warren saw between two contending models for the National Idea in a way that bloodless debate could never accomplish. The southern Mind, Warren argued, was shaped by its great denial of the reality of slavery and its refusal to see defeat in the Civil War as connected to its labor economics and social structures. He labeled this cultural myth the Great Alibi. He was harsh on subscribers to it:

> By the Great Alibi, pellagra, hookworm, illiteracy, mortgages and the other traditional scourges of the South are all explained away or converted into badges of distinction. Laziness is interpreted as the esthetic sense, blood lust rising from boredom and resentful misery as a high sense of honor, and ignorance as divine revelation. By the Great Alibi the Southerner makes his Big Medicine. He turns defeat into victory, defects into virtues. Even more pathetically, he turns his great virtues into absurdities—sometimes vicious absurdities. (L 85)

If Warren had himself been shifty in his thinking about slavery in "The Briar Patch" and *John Brown* (he was), by the time he wrote *The Legacy of the Civil War* he acknowledged that "slavery loom[ed] up mountainously and [could not] be talked away" (RH 7). Talking slavery into the background of the National Mind was the doubtful achievement of the romantic unionism of the Founders, who postponed the reckoning through a series of political compromises. More recently, in the immediate response to *Brown v. Board of Education* (1954), the practitioners of the Great Alibi had used lost cause fog to mobilize a retrograde and "pathetic" insistence on the mythic past. He meant to wrestle the memory of the Civil War away from them, but not in the *Life* text; possibly the popular national weekly was deemed not to be the forum for direct action. He called out particular offenders in the Random House text:

> Does [the southerner] ever realize that the events of Tusca-
> loosa, Little Rock, and New Orleans are nothing more than
> an obscene parody of the meaning of his history? It is a
> debasement of his history, with all that was noble, coura-
> geous, and justifying bleached out, drained away. Does the
> man who, in the relative safety of mob anonymity, stands
> howling vituperation at a little Negro girl being conducted
> into a school building, feel himself at one with those gaunt,
> barefoot, whiskery scarecrows who fought it out, breast to
> breast, to the death, at the Bloody Angle at Spotsylvania,
> in May, 1864? Can the man howling in the mob imagine
> General R. E. Lee, csa, shaking hands with Orval Faubus,
> Governor of Arkansas? (RH 57)

Even Warren, as strongly as he might warn us against the am-
nesiac powers of the Great Alibi, is not immune to the rhetorical force of the heroic narrative, for in this passage he invokes
the heroic dead and Robert E. Lee to rebuke those southern
politicians of the present who have dragged the region into the
futile political strategy of massive resistance to public school
integration, which reinforces a cultural politics that stereotypes
the South as a failed region and turns its traditions into "vicious absurdities."

For Warren the North was likewise doomed by a great simplistic abstraction: the Treasury of Virtue. The Treasury of
Virtue derived from the belief—also a blindness of the magni-
tude of the Great Alibi—that Higher Law had conferred a mo-
nopoly of virtue on the advocates of Union and Abolition, "a
plenary indulgence for all sins past, present, and future, freely
given by the hand of history" (L 85). Those who fancy themselves funded by the Treasury of Virtue forget "that the Repub-
licans [Lincoln's party] were ready in 1861 to guarantee slav-

ery in the South as payment for a return to the Union . . . that the Emancipation Proclamation freeing slaves was limited and provisional, widely disapproved in the North and, as Lincoln admitted, of doubtful constitutional warrant" (L 85). Their liberal descendant in 1961, "the spiritual stockholder who lives on the income of the Treasury of Virtue" (L 85)—perhaps the author of the essay in *The Nation*—will look with scorn upon segregation in Little Rock or New Orleans but suffer myopia when he surveys the South Side of Chicago or Harlem (L 85).

Both absolutes, southern denial and the northern claim to a higher law, had worked together to abolish the pragmatic middle. It was the Great Alibi in collusion with the Treasury of Virtue (inflexible and mutually exclusive ideologies) that had ignited the shooting in 1861. Ordinary citizens, Warren claims, had had enough and were "confirmed in [their] preference for a political system of coalition and compromise, which had broken down in 1860" (L 84–85). At the centennial, "coalition and compromise" were approaching another breaking point. While there was a lot Warren did not like about the white mobs shouting against school desegregation, there was just as much he regretted about the conformist, consumerist, gray-flannel-suited, Soviet-obsessed United States of 1961. Warren did not want the centennial to be remembered by two separate and divided sides, each with its own version of events; nor did he want it to be packaged by Madison Avenue and sold as historical tourism. He wanted complexity worthy of inner turmoil.

There were ways to connect across the gulf of contending cultural politics. If there were two Minds about the Civil War, there was one Body. "Blood is the first cost [of war]," Warren reminded his readers in 1961. "History is not melodrama [*pace* Edmund Wilson], even if it usually reads like that. It was real blood, not tomato catsup or the pale ectoplasm of statistics, that wet the ground at Bloody Angle and darkened the waters of Bloody Pond. . . . But beyond this shock and pathos of the death of 600,000 men, men who really died and in ways they would scarcely have chosen, what has the loss of blood meant, if anything, in the development of the country?" (RH 50). Warren had an answer: remembering "real blood" would jolt a nation of "other-directed" conformists into being individuals again, inspired by the "grandeur" of "our Homeric period" (RH 82; L 87). While this rings as somberly nationalistic and patriotic, epic rather than tragic, it faintly echoes the whiteness politics of amnesia David Blight detected at the end of fifty years of reunion politics during the semicentennial. Testimony to the power of the myth is what Warren is deeply intent on avoiding, yet he is still drawn into its orbit. By glorifying what happened on the fields of battle, one inevitably mutes what happened before the war, when reasons for the war were accumulating, and after, when outcomes were solidified—for a time—in amendments to the Constitution abolishing slavery, conferring citizenship, and guaranteeing the right to vote. Even Warren could succumb to the heroic, narrative escape, as he does when, in the early stages of the *Life* text, he swiftly admits that slavery was a "mountainous" evil but just as swiftly dispatches it: "Once slavery was out of the way, a new feeling about union was possible" (L 82). Like so many in race isolation chambers (the Catton of the Woolson eulogy, some members of the Civil War Centennial Commission), Warren seemed not to see that the new feeling of unity emerging out of the Civil War was reserved for white men who bonded over the shared experience of warfare and tragedy, which muted or erased altogether the fuller and louder meaning of the war. "Together," Warren wrote, "the farm boy of Illinois and the gutter rat of the Mackerelville section of New York shot it out against some Scot of the Valley of Virginia or a Jew from Louisiana" (L 82). Perhaps these examples of regional Americans are not drawn from the officer class, but they are all white. In the Random House version, Warren added a Minnesota trapper and moved the Illinois farm boy to Ohio, but the racial uniformity stayed the same (RH 13). White Americans redefined nationhood by getting to know other white Americans. The centennial was made from these racial omissions and exclusions, even when the stated intention, by as strong-minded a thinker as Warren, was otherwise.

Warren reminded his readers that Civil War–themed propaganda dominated World War II, and he felt a more potent need to return to it in the Cold War of the 1950s: "The turning to the Civil War is, however, a more significant matter than the manipulations of propaganda specialists, and their sometimes unhistorical history. When a people enters upon a period of crisis it is only natural that they look back upon their past and try to find therein some clue to their nature and their destiny" (RH 79). The "crisis" Warren sensed, however, was not the looming civil rights movement, which would call upon a different Civil War memory (memories of emancipated slaves, for example) for a significantly different gallery of heroes and meanings not included in Warren's "Homeric" image, but the Cold War with Russia (RH 101).[21] He worried that Civil War forgetfulness, fostered by progressivist histories of the United States and more currently by the prosperity of the 1950s (prodded as it was by advertising campaigns touting the comforts of conformism in consumption), had left Americans too soft for a confrontation with the USSR:

> In our world of restless mobility, where every Main Street looks like the one before and the throughway is always the same, of communication without communion, of the ad-man's nauseating surrogate for family sense and community in the word *togetherness,* we look back nostalgically on the romantic image of some right and natural relation of man to place and man to man, fulfilled in worthy action. The corrosive of historical realism cannot quite disenthrall us of this,

nor can our hope that somehow in our modern world we may achieve our own new version, humanly acceptable, of identity and community. In fact, the old image may feed our new hope. (RH 92)[22]

Warren was not alone in detecting the pressure of the Cold War present on the Civil War past. A few months before the abbreviated version of *The Legacy of the Civil War* appeared in *Life* magazine, *Look* (*Life's* competitor in the national weekly market) ran MacKinlay Kantor's counterfactual novella *If the South Had Won the Civil War* (1960), hyped by a full-color cover photograph of a bugle draped with the Confederate battle flag.[23] Unlike Warren, who saw the history of the Civil War as real and pragmatic, Kantor decided that the historical Civil War could be reimagined and his counterfactual version used to resolve the constitutional problem of states' rights and the moral and political problem of slavery, continuing in the present as the push for civil rights. Kantor imagined (as other authors of counterfactual histories have before and since) an alternate history in which Lee led the South to victory on the battlefield—Grant having succumbed to a head injury suffered in a fall from a horse during the Vicksburg campaign. In Kantor's version, the Civil War ends in surrender by a confused and leaderless Union; the historical facts of starvation and desertions in Lee's army are quietly expunged from historical memory. The South takes over the Capitol at Washington, D.C., and the U.S. government is exiled to Columbus, Ohio. The CSA annexes Cuba, and Texas temporarily joins the Confederacy. All seems well in the détente following the South's victory until Texas secedes from the CSA over the policy of gradualist integration of emancipated slaves put forward by President Lee.

The two world wars bring the four North American nations closer together. Inevitably, Kantor's alternate history argues, the three nations "consolidate" to face the threat of Soviet Russia. Foreclosed from partnering with Cuba since the South had annexed it, Russia had installed missiles in its Alaskan territories; Kantor proved to be prophetic about a missile threat, he just got the geography wrong. By the time of Kantor's reimagined present, differences over racial integration, reduced to a mere fraction of their intensity in real history, had been worked through in an already completed alternate history in which Lee's gradualist policies had eventually worked. The counterfactual past, then, renders the real present, fraught with civil rights agitation, moot. Kantor brings us to an alternate status quo in 1960 without suffering for the "romantic unionism" Warren skewered, and without the bloody payback for slavery and segregation everyone since Thomas Jefferson had seen coming. In fact, Kantor uses his counterfactual history to argue the politics of gradualism, popular among many white moderates and liberals of the time, for his alternate history "demonstrates" (by the retroactive logic of the genre) that go-slow integration would have resulted in racial harmony if we had followed it from 1865 onward. In Kantor's alternate America, there would be no need for Martin Luther King Jr. Operating with the "logic" of the counterfactual, the politics of deferral will work now, in 1960. The "very long time" Bruce Catton solemnly foretold as the duration for correcting our racial politics had, miraculously, already achieved its promise by 1960. One of the comforts of alternate history as a genre, Kantor's novella shows, is the reassurance that a certain politics *of* the present will already have worked; the "proof" comes in the form of (what now might be termed) a "simulation" of history.[24]

Warren did not imagine an alternate history of the Civil War, but he did try to imagine his way into the turmoil through fiction. His novel *Wilderness: A Tale of the Civil War* (1961) was not one of his successes, neither with reviewers at the time nor with readers and critics since.[25] Whatever its literary shortcomings, *Wilderness* is still a token of the seriousness with which

Warren regarded the Civil War one hundred years after it had occurred; he still felt that the war's narrative presence—the story shape it occupied in the American imagination and memory—was not solely the domain of the fabulist. In both texts of *The Legacy* he had written: "The War grows in our consciousness, larger than life, inexhaustible in its sibylline significance and portentous richness. We shall not be able to fully analyze this richness, but we feel we must try. We must try because it is a way of understanding our own deeper selves, and that need to understand ourselves is what takes us, always, to the deeper contemplations of art, literature, religion and history" (L 87; RH 81).

In *American Oracle*, David W. Blight suggests we read *Wilderness* in the context of Herman Melville's *Battle-Pieces* (1866), poems exploring the deep transformations to the soul of the nation wrought by a war that far outran expectations of its destructiveness. But Nathaniel Hawthorne's "My Kinsman, Major Molineux" (1831) seems a more proximate template. Warren discussed the story often in his criticism and found in it a fittingly complex allegory of the transformation of "romantic unionism" into tumultuous history.

"My Kinsman, Major Molineux" is set in New England during the unrest before the revolution against King George III breaks out into open shooting. Robin, the protagonist, is an archetypal young man who leaves his domestic surround, where its stability, care, and moral traditions muffle the building political unrest, for the epicenter of that unrest: the city. There he encounters waves of disorder: a nocturnal bit of mayhem that seems to mirror the Boston Tea Party, the tarring and feathering of a Crown official, various temptations to drink and engage in sexual activities, and—perhaps the most threatening—invitations to nihilism or cynicism. In the end Robin finds himself in a ruined and empty church, where a seemingly benign gentleman asks Robin what he thinks of the experiences he has undergone in the long night of the allegory. Robin, clearly puzzled and overwhelmed because he is still too naive to realize he has experienced much of anything, asks for directions back to the ferry that brought him to the city. The gentleman politely declines, with the clear implication that once experience starts, one has to ride it to the end. There is, in Warren's favored vocabulary, no reversing history.

Wilderness begins in Europe in 1863 with the angst of Adam Rosenzweig, an idealistic Bavarian Jew who, like Hawthorne's Robin, is barely out of his teens and who is cut off from his traditions (the "identity and community" Warren so highly prized) by the death of his father. The death of fathers was not a new theme for Warren. It might even have been his signature, for the vacancy left by the departed father/Father is a huge psychic void into which the son projects his cultural, personal, sexual, and political anxieties.[26] In "My Kinsman, Major Molineux," Robin represents the adolescent American colonies in the process of leaving the "household" of the British king. Using the allegory of the departed son, Warren explored what he called the "inwardness" of the Civil War, the subject matter of "deeper contemplations" (L 88, 87). In a literary sense, Adam is a wandering ethical conviction in search of historical confirmation in experience. Adam's father, like Warren's, had devoted his life to writing poetry but had never achieved success. The elder Rosenzweig pledged himself to the rights of man and the liberation of secular virtue from the bonds of religious orthodoxy; had he been American he would have been a convert to the church of "romantic unionism." He abandoned his son Adam, village, synagogue, Jewish elders, and moved to Berlin, where he fought in the liberation struggles of 1848. Leopold Rosenzweig lost his battle against political oppression. He limped home to his Bavarian village after a prison sentence when the uprisings of 1848 failed, and on his deathbed he knuckled under to the Law of Jehovah, in the person of Adam's uncle, who pressured his own brother (in Adam's presence) to renege on his faith in secular, human justice.

Adam's shame is as huge as the surrounding mountains, and no sooner is his father's body in its grave and his uncle's brow-beating words echoing in his ears than Adam is on a ship bound from Bremen to New York carrying mercenaries recruited to fight for the Union in the American Civil War. *Soldiers recruited for a fee,* Warren underlines—his novel's first attack upon what, in *The Legacy of the Civil War*, Warren had called the Treasury of Virtue, the northern assumption that their aims were pure, untainted by baser motives like bounties. Adam dreams of fighting for freedom, not for money, and it does not matter to him that the recruiters and recruits have money rather than idealism on their minds as the ship plows the Atlantic. But Adam was born with a deformed foot, for which he had to wear a prosthetic brace. When the recruiters, too drunk initially to notice his limp, discover the deformity—one that will disallow their commission—they threaten to ship Adam back once they dock in New York.

Adam lands in New York in July 1863 and with the help of a sympathetic crew member avoids being returned to Europe. The city Adam enters is as dark and bloody as the allegorical city Hawthorne's Robin strolls into at the advent of the Revolution. Blood has been shed at Gettysburg scarcely a week before Adam's arrival, and draft riots are underway in New York City. Warren does not construct an alternate history for the Civil War; he emphasizes a set of Civil War events taking place far from the Homeric fields of conflict. The first New Yorker Adam meets is a mutilated and lynched African American whose body hangs from a lamppost. In *Wilderness* the Civil War is not a showy pageant of patriotic virtue; it is, rather, moral and political bedlam similar to, if more intense than, the chaotic town that swallows up Robin in Hawthorne's tale.

Adam is swept up, again like Hawthorne's Robin, in the

surges of the riot and finds himself trapped in a dark cellar rapidly filling up with water channeled there by the rioters. A black arm attached to a human being Adam never fully sees pulls him up and out of danger, and he awakens in the prosperous home of an earlier émigré from his own native village—a contact to whom, coincidentally, he has a letter of introduction. From this point on, too many coincidences weigh down Warren's story. Adam's rich contact has recently lost his only son at Chancellorsville, where Confederate forces overwhelmed the Union lines. The deeply grieving man, who has suffered the loss of his wife as well, offers to become Adam's surrogate father. But Aaron Blaustein, the wealthy, sonless merchant, is a complicated impostor in the allegory (like many of the purported aid-givers in Hawthorne's allegory), one who seeks to douse Adam's idealism with torrents of his own nihilism, to tell Adam what the lessons of experience mean before he undergoes them. Blaustein used to believe in God, he says, but now believes only in secular history. History is just what happens to people, says Aaron (not Moses, who brought the law from Sinai on carved tablets); it contains none of the meaning Adam is hungry for: "'Do you know what History is?' Aaron Blaustein demanded. . . . '[I]t is the agony people have to go through . . . so that things will turn out as they would have turned out anyway'" (77). But Adam is resolute; he will go south and fight for freedom, "*Für die Freiheit*" (71), undo his father's shame, and find that things do not turn out "as they would have turned out anyway" but according to a design commensurate to the innate seriousness of human nature in search of meaning to existence.

Blaustein, who made his fortune selling dry goods in the South, fits Adam into a sutler's crew with the black man who rescued him from the flooded cellar, Mose Talbutt, and a white southern exile, Jedeen Hawksworth. Hawksworth's public reputation projects him as an idealistic abolitionist, but his backstory, revealed later in *Wilderness,* is that he fled the South after witnessing his father's kowtowing to a local slaveholding nabob. Clearly, he functions as an alter ego to Adam. Hawksworth, in filial shame—not, Warren points out, in abolitionist fervor—then publicly defied the slaveholding elite by testifying for a runaway slave (Mose Talbutt) in an open southern court. Warren's recurrent plan in *Wilderness* is to make a "wilderness" of the moral and psychological terrain supposed by absolutists on both sides to be simple and unambiguous, then to people it with impostors who seek to steer Adam into dead ends in his quest for meaning. The psychological allegory eventually overwhelms the historical vehicle in Warren's novel. In Hawthorne's tale, Robin's search for meaning in his allegorical journey to the Revolutionary city, played out against the silhouette of the Revolutionary War, takes place within the relatively more compact arc of a short story. Warren ambitiously chose to project his idea of the national search for meaning in the history of the Civil War on the larger scale of the novel.

Adam stands for the remembering community in 1961, looking in the direction of idealism when history is barreling down on him from his blind side. At every turn in the plot Adam is confronted by figures who are not what they claim to be, and the war they are fighting is not a noble endeavor but haphazard slaughter. A Union Medal of Honor winner, for example, is nothing more than a drunken, racist bully who forces freedmen to "bob" for greenbacks in a suffocating tub of flour. A pair of gravediggers, clearly kidnapped from Shakespeare, scrounge the not-yet-hallowed ground of Gettysburg digging up corpses just to rifle their pockets. Mose Talbutt is literally not who he says he is, not a slave who has suffered the lashes of a cruel master but a deserter from a Union army labor crew. Two women Adam encounters tempt him to domestic, sexual detours from the main route of his quest.

At the center of the thematic tangle of *Wilderness*, the moment in which Adam thinks he has meaning figured out, he is as far from it as he was at the beginning. At night, hearing in an adjoining tent a "moaning" he takes to be Mose snoring, Adam consoles himself with the thought that in the morning Mose will forgive him for insulting remarks made when he learned that Mose was not the noble slave he claimed to be. He also hopes to learn that Mose extending a rescuing hand in the flooding cellar was evidence of innate human good, not part of a plan for Mose's survival with Adam as its central object (224). But, of course, Adam is wrong about all of it. In the morning Mose is gone, and Hawksworth is found murdered; the moaning Adam had so confidently taken to be Mose snoring could have been the last living sounds of Hawksworth, killed by Mose.

The hectic climax of the novel is set in the Battle of the Wilderness, May 5–7, 1864: Grant's first move in the war of attrition that culminated at Appomattox not quite one year later. There were twenty-eight thousand casualties on both sides in the Battle of the Wilderness. Union and Confederate soldiers fought in such intimate quarters that many fell by "friendly fire." Hawthorne's use of the charivari of the Boston Tea Party as the allegorical setting for Robin's moral and political confusion is modest in comparison, as Warren probably well knew. Unlike Robin, who merely sees violence (battery, not killing), Adam finally does kill a rebel; but not, Warren is at pains to explain, *"Für die Freiheit."* Adam kills a Confederate soldier after both Blue and Gray troops blunder through the clearing where he has parked his sutler's wagon. He does so not to save himself but to strike a blow for fair play, like a referee in a boxing match, when a scarecrow in gray points a rifle at an unsuspecting Union soldier. Warren's point, for the novel and for the centennial, is that war does not automatically or unambiguously confer heroic status on its participants or meaning on their actions. War, like history, happens to people, and those people and their witnessing descendants must face their history responsibly, not retreat into comfortable and simplistic myths like the Great Alibi or the Treasury of Virtue.

Warren, in *The Legacy of the Civil War* and in *Wilderness*, saw the Civil War, from the perspective of a century later, as big and sturdy enough to support a dense, often overdetermined allegorical narrative of an American journey to self-discovery. That his novel has not fared well with critics is less important, in the present context, than that it functions as an emblem of Warren's insistence on complexity and weight in remembering the Civil War. He felt that a sufficient national, regional, and racial "communion" had not been completed between 1861 and 1961, that the "inner conflict" of race and region was coming up on another collision point, the centennial, and that he was not going to let the last of the last chances at living remembrance go by without connecting the dots from 1861 to 1961 with something more complex than parades and pageants. The allegory embedded in *Wilderness* is heavy, perhaps even baroque, but Warren was struggling against legions of oversimplifiers.

As the centennial wound down, the oversimplifiers seemed to win. Compare the plot of the film *Major Dundee* (1965) with *Wilderness*.[27] U.S. Army major Amos Dundee (Charlton Heston) has been banished to superintend a prisoner of war camp in New Mexico Territory during the Civil War for an unspecified error committed during the Battle of Gettysburg. It is strongly implied that his error was being smarter, or at least more stubborn, than his commanding officer. Among the Confederate prisoners he supervises is a squad captained by Ben Tyreen (Richard Harris). Dundee and Tyreen, like the regions they represent, have an intertwined history. The two had attended West Point together, but before the war Dundee voted to cashier Tyreen from the U.S. Army for participating in a duel. For Tyreen the southerner, the duel was an affair of honor; for Dundee the Yankee, it was a plain violation of army regulations. Thus are the cultural types, Great Alibi and Treasury of Virtue, superficially set up.

The guards at the prisoner of-war-camp, largely composed of ex-slaves, are led by Aesop (Brock Peters). Dundee's relationship with the Colored Troops is official and distant (that is, to Dundee they are soldiers not persons), while Tyreen's is personal albeit condescending: he addresses the freedmen by their first names, not by rank. Some of the members of Tyreen's squad, however, who are portrayed as less favorably socially placed than their captain, are much more prone to racist taunts even though they themselves are prisoners. Tyreen's men, in short, act out the roles of the southerners who harassed black school children in Little Rock, New Orleans, and elsewhere.

This tableau of the status quo in the United States in the early 1960s is complicated by an external threat of a "renegade" Apache, Charriba, who flees across the border into Mexico after killing white American settlers and burning their homes. Mexico is garrisoned at the time by French troops under the command of Emperor Maximilian, whose government is reluctant to aid the United States in its efforts to capture the Apache. Dundee is, nevertheless, ordered to apprehend Charibba, but he cannot carry out the order unless he violates international law by invading a sovereign nation. Seeing that the rebel prisoners have nothing to lose and only have parole or freedom to win, Tyreen pledges himself and his men to form part of a unified force to illegally enter Mexico and capture or kill the Apache. Faced with a foreign enemy, Charriba the Apache, and French troops standing on international law, the interracial and regionally unified force bands together in the hunt for the terrorist.

The North-South, black-white coalition goes well enough, until one of Tyreen's rebel soldiers orders Aesop, the black sergeant of the Colored Troops, to act the valet and remove his boots for him. Aesop refuses and looks to Dundee for support.

Dundee hesitates, defers to Tyreen, who defuses the situation but loses face before his southern troops. He blames Dundee, and their mutual distrust grows deeper. The fault line, if the screenplay were read allegorically, is created by a conflict about whose status is to be debited so that Aesop and his free troops may be equal. Dundee acts as if he controls the Treasury of Virtue and needs only to affirm the law, leaving the altering of hearts and minds to the southerners. Tyreen clearly disagrees; his actions argue that he feels squeezed between federal regulations (Dundee) and the cultural mores of his southern people.

The plot moves on from this episode to introduce the female lead, Teresa (Senta Berger), who has somehow landed in Durango, Mexico, after marrying an Austrian doctor in Vienna. Her husband has been executed for treating rebels fighting against French occupation before the Americans appeared, so she is free for romantic scenes with both Harris and Heston. She chooses Heston but reverses her choice when she discovers that Dundee, left behind to recover from a wound in his upper thigh, takes an indigenous woman as a concubine. Teresa confronts him and leaves—but not for Tyreen.

After a series of exploits against apparently hapless French lancers, what is left of Dundee's expeditionary force (minus Teresa, who cannot cope with the dark, brooding, and never-disclosed secret in Dundee's soul) captures Charriba and begins the dangerous retreat back across the border. Eventually they are blocked from crossing the Rio Grande into the United States by a column of French cavalry. A diversion is called for to give the American soldiers time to cross to safety. Tyreen, mortally wounded in the first unsuccessful attempt to ford the river, invokes HONOR for one last time. Waving his plumed hat with appropriate, and suicidal, flair, he rides into the column of French soldiers, confounding them just long enough for the Americans to wade to safety. He dies looking northward toward the United States.

The director's cut of *Major Dundee* runs 152 minutes, and much of the story could be read, in 1965, as American criticism of French misadventure in Vietnam that precipitated U.S. involvement there or as a vehicle for igniting some "screen chemistry" between Heston and Berger. Most of the chemistry, as it was in David Lean's *Lawrence of Arabia* (1962), percolates between the male leads, Harris and Heston, whose relationship in the script tracks Civil War cliché to a hackneyed ending. *Major Dundee* aims its message through a thin veneer of Civil War history at an American public ready to believe that federally backed policies of equality for African Americans (civil rights and voting rights legislation had been signed in 1964 and 1965) would work if recalcitrant, lower-class, and irresponsible white southerners did not insist on clinging to outdated racist behaviors: their "vicious absurdities," in Warren's words. The responsibility for achieving harmonious race relations, winning the contest for hearts and minds, *Major Dundee* suggests, rests with the white southern upper class (Tyreen). Beyond enacting civil rights and voting legislation, there is little or nothing federal enforcement (Dundee) can do.

By 1965, according to David W. Blight, the American public was beset with "Centennial fatigue." *Major Dundee* could be seen as an ideal example of the symptoms: a wide array of plotlines from the moderately serious to the farcical, a gorgeous and exotic actress, the assurance that American troops are smarter and kinder than those of any foreign country, and a gesture to the U.S. politics of race that, by the end of the 152 minutes, has been digested by our brave but ragtag troops vanquishing an enemy abroad. The last of the last chances at Civil War memory molts into more contemporary anxieties and creaky romantic cliché.

CHAPTER THREE

The Civil War and Its Afterlife

In memoriam, Noel Polk (1943–2012)

In the first volume of Will Shetterly and Vince Stone's *Captain Confederacy* (2007), the eponymous superhero is a strapping blond hunk in tights, with the Confederate battle flag stretched across his rippling pectorals. He looks like a pickup truck in red, white, and blue spandex. His partner is blonde and buxom Miss Dixie, a Confederate Wonder Woman without the tiara and Lasso of Truth. Following the standard superhero trope, they hide a secret identity but not in an effort to preserve their daytime personae. Far from being mild-mannered regular citizens by day, they are puppets of a propaganda machine within a Confederate government, a century and a half (or more) since its triumph in the Civil War, a regime that, in order to survive in the twenty-first century, broadcasts phony episodes of black on white crime so that the Captain and Miss Dixie can be filmed performing "real" rescues.

The sesquicentennial takes place in *Captain Confederacy*, in an era of elaborate charades and reality television. Lives are not lived but performed. The Captain and Miss Dixie are in fact cordial friends with the actors who portray their black nemeses, Blacksnake and Kate. Between episodes the four hang out and kvetch about how much they hate the forced deception and fakery of their jobs, and by the third or fourth page they brew up a plot to break free of their bosses and expose the big lie. *Captain Confederacy* (vol. 1) then embarks on a complicated set of plot steps in which the four superheroes attempt to "secede" from governmental control. By the end of volume 1, only Kate (the black female superhero), Jeremy Gray (the actor who plays Captain Confederacy), and Roxanne Lee (the niece of the current President Lee of the CSA and the actress who plays Miss Dixie) are left standing. The actor who plays Blacksnake, and who never wholeheartedly agreed with the plan, is killed in a shootout with CSA secret police. Kate and Jeremy, after surviving several assassination attempts, and in Jeremy's case death itself, have fallen in love.[1] Evading the secret police, the lovers propose a new myth for the Confederacy to the current President Lee, and she presents them on Confederate television as the new heroic pair. Kid Dixie supplants Miss Dixie, and Kate, an African American woman, becomes the next Captain Confederacy (155–56). Transformation is the theme of the new era; genders and races shift places and roles. One thing does not change much: Blacksnake, the African American male, seems indigestible to the theme of trans-formation, and he is eliminated. *Captain Confederacy* might be shelved under "Fantasy and Science Fiction," but the author and artist, Will Shetterly and Vince Stone, have uncovered one strategy for remembering the Civil War in the latter days of its sesquicentennial: alternate history or the counterfactual mode.

In a brief afterword to volume 1, Shetterly explains some of the design and thinking behind his alternate history of the Confederacy. His commentary bolsters the theme of transformation. Although web sources place Shetterly in Minnesota now, he writes that he was born and raised in the South and that his family "took part in the struggle for civil rights" (157). But he is not interested in the history of the South (what *did* happen); rather, the malleability of alternate histories rivets his attention. In one possible history, "[a] modern-day CSA could have become an enlightened nation. The economics of slavery and the pressure of international disapproval would have made the Confederacy abandon slavery by the 1870s or '80s, and a victorious Confederacy would have treated its former slaves better than a crushed South did" (157). "Or," Shetterly continues, shifting to another variant, "a victorious Confederacy might have become a place far worse than the one here [in *Captain Confederacy*]. The human instinct to resent meddling by outsiders could have produced a CSA that clung to slavery well into the Twentieth Century. In the game of If, anything is possible" (157).[2] Not "anything," I would like to argue, in rebuttal to Shetterly's theory about "the game of If." Although much is possible to the imagination, even to an imagination not influenced by computer-generated imagery, the widest range of "anything" is not. We indulge in alternate history for the very same or similar reasons we pursue social or collective memory. What happened in our past supplies us with definite narratives (Shetterly's thumbnail reference to "the struggle for civil rights" is one), which we are not at total liberty to abandon. Those narratives might not universally satisfy the needs of those contemplating the South in the present days of the historical continuum. Collective memory covers the negotiations between what *did* happen and what we would prefer to remember. I have discussed these negotiations as they were conducted at the semicentennial and centennial in the two previous essays. Our encounter with the Civil War 150 years after Appomattox is of a piece with our previous encounters in that we negotiate the content and form of memory. What is distinctive now is the influence of the counterfactual mode in our negotiations with the past.

The plot of *Captain Confederacy II* (2012) follows Kid Dixie and Captain Confederacy to New Orleans, where they are scheduled to participate in a superhero Olympics sponsored by the NAUF, the North American Unity Foundation, a nefarious mutation of the secret media forces that controlled reality in volume 1. In the alternate history backstory to *Captain Confederacy*, the American Civil War ended, after two years, in a negotiated truce. The Confederacy retained its capitol in Richmond (and the presidency stayed in the Lee family), but the United States, as it had in MacKinlay Kantor's *If the South Had Won the Civil War*, moved west to Columbus, Ohio. Since, in the alternate aftermath of no-Appomattox, the United States did not develop in the nineteenth century as a world power but continued as separate and competitive geocultural fragments, the empires and regimes the United States of recorded history had vanquished (Imperial Japan and the Third Reich) still wield world influence in the counterfactual present of *Captain Confederacy*. The imagined present of *Captain Confederacy* is, then, a quilted landscape of national-cultural entities. A Nippon Empire with an outpost in California and a Germany that apes Second World War propaganda stereotypes dominate the global map. In the alternate North America (in addition to the NAUF, which is headquartered in the Northeast), there is a "Free Louisiana" apparently run by a sophisticated mulatto cohort bilingual in French and English, a Native American region known as "The Great Spirit Alliance" that stretches across the upper Midwest, a desert empire descended from Mormon settlements and using the former historical name for that empire—"Deseret," the Republic of Texas, Mexico, the People's Republic of California, and "Pacifica" running northward across Oregon and Washington State. Each constituency sends a typical champion to New Orleans for a competitive spectacle that turns out to be a charade. The NAUF, aiming to spark violence among the various regionalities so that it, with the clandestine backing of Nippon and Germany, can step into the chaos and impose order and control, manipulates the competition. The putsch fails thanks to Captain Confederacy, Kid Dixie, and their superhero posse made up of champions from the other regions. Save for a few superheroes who are killed—the representatives of Germany and Texas—the status quo is restored, and yet again a conspiracy is thwarted.

Captain Confederacy is not shy about its borrowings from American popular superhero comics and conspiracy classics: *The Manchurian Candidate* and the Batman epic seem to be its closest reservoirs of plot twists and characters. Leaving character appropriations and plot borrowings aside for the time being, let's consider the *place* of the South in *Captain Confederacy*, its geocultural shuffling of the Mason-Dixon Line. Surrounded not by states with political and historical origins but by less fixed regions defined by ethnic groups and their stereotypical lifestyles, the South in *Captain Confederacy* is drawn as an apocalyptic, postmodern, urban wasteland, with familiar forms of southern racism on the rural fringe (white hayseeds in bib overalls who make sexually explicit comments to a black woman, a Klan-type family proud of bombing churches), which serve as an homage to the stereotypes of cultural history. The central image of the South of *Captain Confederacy* (the modern city where its government and media are headquartered) is anything but traditionally "southern"; the Richmond of "the game of IF" is a metaphorical geography where the civic pact has deteriorated almost to the point of disappearance, global corporations control economies and politics for their own profit from high-rise boardrooms, and citizens walk the concrete urbanscape in a desensitized stupor. Has the social and historical data identifying the South of our previous Civil War commemorations morphed into a library of computer-generated images and focus-group clichés? Are we now displaced from the South that anchored "the struggle for civil rights" and set adrift in the postmodern no-place characterized by historian James Cobb as "the irrevocably assimilated and indistinguishable No South"?[3] Has the anxiety felt by some of the centennial celebrants in 1961—the fear that with the passing of the last surviving human connection to the Civil War, we have or soon will lose the capacity to remember it altogether—come to an ultimate, inescapable, and dark fruition? Does anyone care?

To answer any one of these questions we need to ask a simpler one first: where is the South now? Very few of our predecessors, those citizens of the United States in 1911 and in 1961, would have taken that question seriously—they all knew. The South did not shapeshift. Quentin Compson's 1909 rail journey back to Mississippi from Harvard in *The Sound and the Fury* (1929) is the literary expression of a sociological map with real demarcations; the South is arguably the only "place" in Faulkner's novel where his doomed hero, Quentin, feels at home with naturalistic clarity:

> The train was stopped [somewhere in Virginia] when I waked and I raised the shade and looked out. The car was blocking a road crossing, where two white fences came down a hill and then sprayed outward and downward like part of the skeleton of a horn, and there was a nigger on a mule in the middle of the stiff ruts, waiting for the train to move. How long he had been there I didn't know, but he sat straddle of the mule, his head wrapped in a piece of blanket, as if they had been built there with the fence and the road, or with the hill, carved out of the hill itself, like a sign put there saying You are home again.[4]

Where is that South now? Gone with the unexamined assumption of Quentin's (and Faulkner's) white supremacy? Or buried under a suburban or exurban mall, as a good deal of Virginia is these days?

The generation of academic scholars whose summary achievement was *The History of Southern Literature* (1985) had been young men and women during the centennial, and their South still claimed an uppercase "S," though some in that cadre could feel tremors.[5] The South was a concrete and documentable lived life for most of the members of this group; it preceded in time its representation in the literature they read and established in a canon in *The History of Southern Literature.* To some this South was a belief system almost metaphysical, to others a census of empirical characteristics of persons and their lives distinctive in history by diet, climate, politics, and religion. The introduction to *The History of Southern Literature* contains the brave assertion of living presence that marks the temper of those times and people: "The facts are that there existed in the past, and there continues to exist today, an entity within American society known as the South, and that for better or for worse the habit of viewing one's experience in terms of one's relationship to that entity is still a meaningful characteristic of both writers and readers who are or have been part of it" (5).

On the metaphysical side, there were the poets and critics of the Fugitive/Agrarian brotherhood whose manifesto *I'll Take My Stand* (1930)—frequently threatened with obsolescence since its initial publication more than eighty years ago—still bobs to the surface of the southern conversation. On the other side were the more empirical chroniclers of the South, followers of Howard Odum or V. O. Key, who measured southerners' diets and incomes, marriage practices, or voting patterns and church attendance. In spite of great differences between these two camps, there was a consensus that the South was an "entity within American society" and, as such, could be distinguished from others by real traits.

That South is still palpable in historian James Cobb's *Away Down South: A History of Southern Identity* (2005). Cobb remembers singing "Dixie" in a Georgia elementary school assembly in the 1950s within that "entity," only later learning that the song was composed (allegedly) by an Ohioan for the New York minstrel stage (1). The lesson for Cobb was that distinctive and exclusive "entities" might be the products of cultural (learned and constructed) perception, and that perception has a history of knowledge and ignorance, fate and choice, memory and amnesia. "I want to emphasize first of all," he writes in his introduction, "that, as it appears here, identity typically refers to a *perception* of reality rather than to reality itself" (6).[6] After pondering the question of southern identity for more than three decades, Cobb reports that he no longer offers a definitive answer when asked if the South still exists (8). Instead, he opts for a "conception of identity without distinctiveness or at least one that emphasizes the importance of being 'oneself or itself' over not being 'another'" (337). The South may still be an identity, but what that identity represents may not be the same to each and every claimant or maintain a static meaning to the same claimant over time.[7]

Even allowing for the fundamental differences between poets and empiricists, partisans on either side up to the generation immediately preceding James Cobb could have told you where the South lay and, almost to the precise degree of latitude and longitude, where it departed alien territory and, as Quentin sensed in Faulkner's novel, became "home." There is a measure of South fatigue hovering in some of Cobb's conclusions but not yet the paranoid suspicion that regional and ethnic antagonism is a fabrication of corporate-controlled media or that "the game of IF" has abolished all the rules, as there is, for example, in *Captain Confederacy*.

For the generation on the cusp of change from entity to perception, Atlanta was the anti-South, the ominous, looming zeroing out of distinctiveness finally accomplished, some still feel, by the 1996 Olympics. For aficionados of this position, the Atlanta Regency Hyatt was the omen of change. Designed by John Portman, an architect born in South Carolina and trained at Georgia Tech, it was the first "atrium hotel" in the world when it opened in 1967, with a revolving restaurant at the top of its twenty-two stories. It was the perennial headquarters hotel for SAMLA, the South Atlantic Modern Language Association, and one doesn't have to imagine much to conjure up the sounds of scholarly papers on southern literature echoing upward every autumn into the hum and drone of the atrium. It moved C. Hugh Holman (another South Carolinian), whose essay "The View from the Regency Hyatt" (1969) is redolent of departing faith in southern distinctiveness seasoned with a faint note of anxiety about its fate in the future. After brief appraisals of the southernness (differences included) in the writings of T. S. Stribling, Erskine Caldwell, Thomas Wolfe, and Flannery O'Connor (all Georgia writers), Holman reaffirms the "distinctive characteristics" of the South as a region: "the presence of the Negro and the shame of his enslavement and second-class citizenship; the historical experience of military defeat, military occupation, and reconstruction; and a predominantly agricultural economy" (107).[8] But this was a vulnerable certainty, for the actual view from the Regency Hyatt (in 1969) was change, change, change: "As tobacco roads give way to interstate highways, as country stores become shopping centers, as small towns become the suburban areas of booming cities, is the South as social subject any longer relevant? Can one take the glass-enclosed elevator to the twenty-second floor of the Regency Hyatt in Atlanta and look out upon a world distinctively different from what he might see in New York, Chicago, or Los Angeles, even if he doesn't glance at the nationally televised game being played in the Falcons' and Braves' splendid new stadium?" (106–7). Holman held out slim hope for an affirmative answer, but today that hope is gone. The Falcons play in the Georgia Dome and the Braves play at Turner Field. The "splendid new stadium" of 1969 is no more. And in the Atlanta of the millennium, you can't see much at all from the Hyatt Regency, twenty-two stories being closer to midrise than highrise these days. The once-distinctive rotating rooftop restaurant, Polaris, is hardly visible in stock photos of the contemporary Atlanta skyline. For a generation of critics who have known little or nothing else than postmodern, postnew Atlanta, the city (if that is what Atlanta is) is the accomplished fact of placelessness as the new normal, the one-size-fits-all megacity of Tom Wolfe's *A Man in Full* (1998) and the dark eminence lurking behind Will Shetterly and Vince Stone's *Captain Confederacy*. We can now answer Hugh Holman's question: yes, every place with a horizon of glass-and-steel towers looks about the same, whether you are on the street or in the penthouse.

If it is a truism that the present is a moment in transition, what does our particular present mean for collective memory, particularly for memory of the Civil War? Where are we on the arc from 1911 that runs through 1961 to the present? Can we, like the author of *Captain Confederacy*, possess one lived memory of the South yet make up another and live in the alternate? Anniversaries are moments that people (in communities of shared identity) deliberately set aside to measure the level of meaning and distance from the present of their (supposedly) shared past, and during anniversaries we pose ourselves the work of getting a grip on history, the inexorable flow of time and change, and of inquiring whether we are in fact who we say we are. For anniversaries we make social memory a ritual, a tool, even a sacrament. We formalize it, set it aside from daily life. We hold memory to be unquestionable truth, even if history offers little or no confirmation that what we remember to have happened actually did happen. In some cases, we construct an alternate history.

Southerners are collectively and durably a people of memory, set against the forces pushing them into the future. W. Fitzhugh Brundage makes the point succinctly in his introduction to *Where These Memories Grow: History, Memory, and Southern Identity* (2000): "Southerners, after all, have the reputation of being among the most historically oriented of peoples and of possessing the longest, most tenacious memories."[9] William Faulkner's enigmatic words in *Requiem for a Nun* (1950), "The past is never dead. It isn't even past," hover over southern memory like a mantra and have found their way into a presidential speech.[10] Or as James Cobb might say, Faulkner's words hover like a cloud of shame and guilt for racist behaviors and ways of thinking that hang on unwanted.[11] Like Brundage, but more particularly to the point of our sesquicentennial, David W. Blight has linked race, memory, and the South in *Race and Reunion: The Civil War in American Memory* (2001) and more recently in *American Oracle: The Civil War in the Civil Rights Era* (2011).[12] Blight assesses Civil War memory not as shared yet essentially personal reminiscences but as a politics that brought about national reunion in the half-century from 1865 to 1915, the first fifty years of Civil War memory, and revisited the centennial with often unwanted divisiveness. Both "reunions," Blight argues, were achieved at the cost of either denying or delaying racial justice, a cause that even in retrospect continues to "roil political issues of today."[13] "As long as we have a politics of race in America," Blight affirms in *Race and Reunion,* "we will have a politics of Civil War memory" (4).[14]

As long as we have a Civil War memory, memory will be the pivot point of the politics of something. But will it always be race? Public memory, unlike the private and personal counterpart, is a memory composed by official selection and consensus: what, when, and how to foster public memory are mostly matters of choice, manipulation, and purpose. Something like the sesquicentennial of the Civil War does not simply break out in improvisation. Entities within the nation—government agencies, cultural groups and societies, heritage organizations—anticipate the anniversary, plan for it, assemble resources, and construct meanings. Or they decide not to plan: the U.S. Congress has declined to establish a national agency or commission for the sesquicentennial of 2011–15.[15]

Given the gridlock in Washington at present and the skittishness about adding to the federal budget, it is probably no wonder that the Senate has preferred not to debate the causes of the war or to appropriate $500,000 per fiscal year for 2012 through 2016 and $3.5 million to the NEH for programming grants. No one would willingly look back on former ceremonies of memory like the centennial, the mineshafts of controversy unforeseen, the sinkholes of unintended consequences and overlooked points of view. The centennial "celebration" of the Civil War is particularly ripe with lessons of how not to plan an anniversary; reliving battlefield valor in the midst of a civil rights movement seems now like an obvious error. It is easy to see our mistakes in hindsight. Blight argues that the semicentennial in 1911–15 was all about consolidating white political and social power in the Progressive Era through the politics of reunion. When the Civil War Centennial Commission set sail in a similar direction half a century later, political power had shifted, and black voices that had been ignored in the 1910s made themselves heard in the 1960s. Some commentators see the present sesquicentennial as taking place in an America different from the one that sponsored the two previous anniversaries, if only in nuance. That is, systemic racism still exists, but the racists themselves are fewer and aging. Or the dark side has found ways to encode its language, leading some commentators to write that "America's changing demographics make some nostalgic for a society in which white Christians were more dominant" or to describe certain strata of our society as riddled with "anxiety about losing majority status."[16] We all know how that message translates. Will the sesquicentennial of the Civil War be written in code?

We don't remember all the past all the time; that would

simply disable us, make the past a virtual present, and we would walk around in it like zombies, the undead of our own past like the cast of 2000 *Maniacs*, who celebrate their Civil War Centennial by killing and eating Yankee tourists.[17] But we do oblige ourselves to remember parts of the past at appointed times, and my curiosity in these essays has been directed at how our thinking at those appointed times is shaped by vocabularies of which we might be only dimly aware—codes of a sort but not always deliberate codes. Conscious intentions might determine when and what to remember, but contemporary vocabularies heavily or lightly encode how we remember. Only the people who lived through the war can remember the war (and many of them wished not to); the rest of us have to settle for substitutes, each of which entails a code—a structure of telling: novels, poems, histories, plays, films, reenactments, orations, lectures. The real war, as Walt Whitman clearly predicted, never got in the books. It did not get into public memory, either—at least not without being altered to the contours of whatever present needed it. The American public's conflicted notions of blood shaped the fiftieth anniversary, and equally conflicted worries about the loss of the past accelerated by political and social change in the present shaped the centennial.

Where are we now? What are the vocabularies (concealed or otherwise) shaping our memory of the sesquicentennial? If *Captain Confederacy* is a valid indicator, we live in a United States more loosely defined by regional characteristics than by state boundaries. The South is being replaced by southerness, a cultural identity based less on history and more on lifestyle— the kind of affect marketed successfully by publications like *Garden & Gun*. There are more certain differences between the present and the pasts of fifty or one hundred years ago. We are no longer a print culture, as we were for the earlier anniversaries of the war. It is not that we don't read at all, but that fewer of us do. Most of us tend to take in text and images visually, on cell phones, e-books, and computer screens. Because we do, we are accustomed to the possibilities of computer-generated images that are indistinguishable from, and often preferable to, the real thing. D. W. Griffith, in his time, was a miracle worker with the battle scenes in *The Birth of a Nation,* but they were all filmed within the limitations of real time and space, and we look at them today as we would look at museum antiquities. As human beings we are limited by time and space, but as consumers of visual images we can experience simulations of reality that are much more persuasive than those available to our ancestors. And we are very prone to do just that: we can, for example, imagine Captain Confederacy as a caped superhero or reimagine Abraham Lincoln as a vampire hunter and the slavery at the heart of the war as nothing more than a household blood bank for the vampires who ran southern plantations.[18]

Our memory of the Civil War in the twenty-first century is already a mediated memorial for another reason. How can we remember the war now without at least an echo of how we remembered it fifty years or a century ago? American public memory of the Civil War, clearly through its first half-century, was poised on a massive fault line where the celebrated memory of warrior valor on both sides ground against the suppressed awareness of postponed promises of racial equality. President Woodrow Wilson gave a hastily drafted speech at the 1913 commemoration held at Gettysburg, hailing the sacrifice on both sides of the pivotal battle there, but more significantly he was the president who screened *The Birth of a Nation* in the White House and who supplied one of the finest taglines of all time, paraphrasing Coleridge's comment on seeing Edmund Kean perform Shakespeare, by calling Griffith's film "history written with lightning."[19]

Those who heard his remarks or read his endorsement of the film were a lot closer to the real war than we are, but they were also a lot closer (perhaps without fully admitting it) to the white racial anxieties that shaped the commemoration.

We might think it just as easy to see the political crack-up of the centennial in the early 1960s, when the narrative of civil rights was much more mature than it had been at the fiftieth anniversary and the narrative of the birth of a (white) nation was showing signs of splintering. The National Park Service apparently possesses a long institutional memory of its part in the debacle. Since so many of the NPS's historical sites are Civil War–related, they constitute the frontline of an ongoing cultural battle. "A large number of our visitors," an NPS author explained in 2008, "come to our battlefields to walk the sacred ground where their ancestors fought."[20] Affirming ancestor worship was the downfall of the public enterprise of commemorating the centennial fifty years ago, so the NPS "decided a new goal would be to address slavery as the main cause of the Civil War" (51). This adjustment to memory irritated some ancestor worshippers who were disinclined to hear, in the twenty-first century, "that slavery 'might' have been a cause of the Civil War" (51). They dispatched over one thousand postcards to the office of the secretary of the interior objecting to the intrusion of history upon memory. The NPS held to its purpose—to learn from the myopia of the centennial—and "From Civil War to Civil Rights" became an early theme in the planning for the sesquicentennial, resulting in books, pamphlets, heritage trails, and lesson plans steering a direct course from the battlefields to the demonstrations.[21] But could the NPS program of commemoration be an example of fighting a bygone culture war rather than the current one?

Organized commemorations of the sesquicentennial seem designed to mitigate pure ancestor worship. The American Library Association, supported by the National Endowment for the Humanities, has sponsored a national discussion program,

Let's Talk About It: Making Sense of the American Civil War,
hosted by public libraries across the country selected for very
modest program grants through a competition. The common
readings are Gwendolyn Brooks's novel *March* (2005), James
McPherson's *Crossroads of Freedom: Antietam* (2002), and a
volume of source and contextual readings edited by historian
Edward L. Ayers.[22] Ayers's selections are aimed at the problems
encountered in past anniversaries: Alexander Stephens's "'Cornerstone' Speech," the Emancipation Proclamation in its full
ambiguity, excerpts from the works of historians presenting the
war as chaotic slaughter rather than valorous warfare, fiction
by Ambrose Bierce and Shelby Foote—all of which could have
been helpful in the 1961 debate. Adding Bobbie Ann Mason's
short story "Shiloh" seems indicative of an awareness that the
cultural climate might have changed.

Does that mean we are honing a new way to remember the
real Civil War? Will it finally get into the books? Has Civil War
memory at last been liberated from the politics of race? For the
rememberers of fifty years ago, the political medium of public
memory was blatant; American racial politics were literally in
the street. For participants in the sesquicentennial, the politics
of Civil War memory are more difficult to track but not impossible.

Old sectional scores still show up in the skirmishes of the
contemporary culture war, as we can see for example in Adam
Goodheart's *1861: The Civil War Awakening* (2011). Goodheart uses his discussion of Lincoln's call for a special session
of the U.S. Congress on July 4, 1861, to take a swipe at the
Confederate Congress meeting then in Richmond: "By con-
trast [with Lincoln's call for the special session], the lacklus-
ter, shopworn rhetoric of the new Southern republic's leading
statesmen was not merely a failure of aesthetics, but proof of
the intellectual poverty and moral laziness undergirding their
entire enterprise. The Confederacy was never really much of

a cause—lost or otherwise. In fact, it might better be called an effect, a retroactive stratagem tarted up with ex post facto justifications."[23] Goodheart's temperamental swipe at a political assembly dead for a century and a half is a sign (if we ever needed one) that Faulkner was right: the past isn't dead, it isn't even past. Is it something that happened 150 years ago that brings Goodheart's rhetoric to boil, or is there a contemporary issue using and shaping memory, perhaps another Congress whose actions and inactions rankle?[24]

In a recent *New York Review of Books* article critical of conservative icons like Rush Limbaugh and Glenn Beck, David Bromwich suggests that the Fox News range of the political opinion spectrum has been infected by an ideological pathogen he calls "The Rebel Germ."[25] Limbaugh is a more active carrier than Beck, Bromwich claims with a mild bow to history, since several of Limbaugh's ancestors in Missouri were supporters of the Confederacy. Bromwich, however, moves on from *ad hominem* arguments to a larger and familiar assertion that the otherwise healthy American body politic has been infected by a hostile organism: first, centuries ago when slavery was introduced and a civil war fought because of it, and more recently in the late twentieth century, when legally condoned racial apartheid ended but the habits lived on in "the southernization of American politics." Bromwich concludes that the encoded racism in our politics "[shows] more plainly now than at any moment since Richard Nixon's 1968 campaign" (4). The "germ" fostering the resurgence of "southernization" in politics, in Bromwich's view, is the familiar combination of states' rights and white superiority but mutated in such a way that carriers of the rebel germ seldom present overt symptoms (4). No one carrying the "germ," for example, would be as frank as Alexander Stephens, vice president of the Confederacy, whose "Cornerstone Speech" of 1861 placed the South against the founding principle of equality: "Our new Government is founded upon exactly the opposite ideas; its foundations are laid, its cornerstone rests, upon the great truth that the negro is not equal to the white man; that slavery, subordination to the superior race, is his natural and normal condition."[26] Robert Penn Warren, in *The Legacy of the Civil War*, and other white southern liberals during the years before Nixon's original southern strategy was deployed in the 1960s, had no trouble finding manifest traces of the "rebel germ" in the politics of "massive resistance" to desegregation. In fact, in *The Legacy of the Civil War* Warren named names: Almond, Faubus, Barnett, governors of Virginia, Arkansas, and Mississippi respectively. Critics like David Bromwich want us to think of "southernization" during the sesquicentennial as having undergone cultural mutation: the germ is still there; its carriers have just figured out codes for evading overt appearances.[27]

In the two previous essays, I assumed that the remembering American publics during the fiftieth and one hundredth anniversaries of the Civil War had less trouble identifying (and fewer inhibitions saying) what they were to remember than we do now, 150 years after the the Civil War. I speculated that they were not fully aware of *how* they did or were to do the remembering. With the two brief contemporary examples mentioned just now (Goodheart and Bromwich), I suggest that in the present climate of political and cultural polarization and gridlock we are coming to use memory not so much to access our past as to stake out and defend ideological positions in the present. Granted that the South of 1911 and the South of 1961 have surrendered to what James Cobb mournfully calls "the irrevocably assimilated and indistinguishable No South" (7), it seems that the *what* and *how* of remembering have been fundamentally changed but not abolished—at least not yet.

Scott Romine, whose *The Real South* (2008) points the way to read the South in our climate of virtual realities, argues that we now have become accustomed to simulations rather than facts, and we are to a degree anesthetized to compromising the *what* by our fascination with the *how*. This compromise is further illustrated by *Captain Confederacy* and *Abraham Lincoln: Vampire Hunter* winning the contest for public memory over a very modest NEH/ALA program of public library discussion groups. Looking for Civil War memory in all the old places might, in our environment of simulations, be a doomed quest. What we're liable to turn up is not the real thing but an array of reenactments, the kind of South Tony Horwitz tours in *Confederates in the Attic* (1999).[28] When the simulation competes with the real thing in an economy where real and counterfeit are nearly indistinguishable, maybe we should turn away from the multivolume history and look at the counterfactual.

One counterfactual chronicle of the Civil War designed to weave together history and ideology is the trilogy of Civil War novels cowritten by Newt Gingrich and William R. Forstchen: *Gettysburg* (2003), *Grant Comes East* (2004), and *Never Call Retreat* (2005).[29] Under a thick blanket of historical verisimilitude, Gingrich and Forstchen simulate a Civil War in which Lee wins the battle of Gettysburg (a staple of the Civil War counterfactual) but makes the fateful error of continuing his Maryland campaign through the late summer and fall of 1863 instead of retreating, as he did in reality, to Virginia: a disastrous decision in that it pulls Grant into the eastern theater of the war months earlier than his actual arrival in the spring of 1864. Grant coming east early becomes paradoxically fortunate, in the Gingrich-Forstchen version, in that it produces a battlefield draw in 1863 rather than the war of attrition of the spring of 1864 to the spring of 1865.

In *Grant Comes East* (the second volume of the trilogy) Lee and the Army of Northern Virginia follow up counterfactual victories at Gettysburg with an assault on Washington, D.C., that almost succeeds and an occupation of Baltimore that proves to be costly and ultimately unsustainable (as did the

U.S. occupation of Baghdad at about the same time Gingrich and Forstchen were writing their trilogy). In the third and final installment of the trilogy, *Never Call Retreat*, Grant and Lee finally meet, not in Virginia but between the Susquehanna and Potomac Rivers west of Baltimore in the late summer of 1863. Lee's goal, of course, is to capture the Capitol, something he achieves in other counterfactuals such as MacKinlay Kantor's *If The South Had Won the Civil War* and Harry Turtledove's *The Guns of the South* (1992).[30] In *Never Call Retreat*, however, Lee never makes it to the streets of Washington; the simulated Civil War ends not with a southern defeat (and the failed political reconstruction of actual history) but rather with a negotiated truce ending an exhausted battlefield stalemate. As well-researched as parts of the Gingrich-Forstchen trilogy seem to be, the clear purpose of the coauthors' adjustment project is not to fill in or correct the historical record but rather to substitute a counterfactual historical "reality" from which to imagine or extrapolate an alternative political present. That present is ours: the present of our polarized politics for which the Civil War is an epic in wish fulfillment.

In *Grant Comes East* Gingrich and Forstchen deploy familiar Civil War themes to cover their adjustments to actual history. One familiar theme is that Union forces, beneficiaries of vast commercial and industrial assets, will unfailingly and ultimately defeat the Confederacy no matter how many different outcomes of battles and campaigns are imagined. (Harry Turtledove, in *The Guns of the South*, overcomes this historical barrier by equipping Lee's army with AK-47s, shipped via time travel from the future to the past.) In fact, the coauthors devote dozens of pages to minute descriptions of Union logistics: miles of track, locomotives, rolling stock, medical supplies, shoes, and shipping schedules—symbols of a thriving industrial economy overwhelming the agrarian, pastoral plantation South. The Union achieves a kind of materialist sublime (*Grant* 238ff).

On the Confederate side, where materiel is admittedly in short supply, pageantry fills the deficit in shoes and ships and sealing wax (*Grant* 256).

What the warring sides have (counterfactually) in common, however, is the politics of emancipation. *Grant Comes East* alters history just enough to suggest that absolute white superiority was the policy of only a faction of the Confederacy (not, as Stephens's "Cornerstone Speech" and the Confederate constitution itself stated, all of it), and had the war ended with the political and military compromise imagined by Gingrich and Forstchen rather than unconditional military surrender, Lee, at heart a pragmatic emancipationist like Lincoln, would have seized the moment to bring about a gradualist end to apartheid in an independent South.[31] In other words, the alternate past might have accommodated states' rights *and* civil rights, and the Civil War–instigated politics of memory might have been a politics nearer to Gingrich's strand of conservatism than to a politics of race. The North could have pursued its kind of centralized federalism, and the South could have produced a more diffuse confederation (although the Gingrich-Forstchen trilogy does not imagine how this postwar would have worked), and the red state / blue state polarization we experience today would not present itself as either/or but rather both/and. And Newt Gingrich, a politician who made New Federalism a signature of his various campaigns (until the Republican presidential primaries of 2012, when he dropped out of the running), would have a history to buttress his idea of the present.

Lincoln, a main character in Civil War counterfactuals from *The Clansman* onward, "controls the narrative" of *Grant Comes East*. First, Gingrich and Forstchen invent Lincoln's relationship with the black majordomo of the White House, a man who, they imagine, has served every president since 1814 and who has named his son Washington Madison Quincy Bartlett (72). "Jim" Bartlett, this presidential valet, functions as

Lincoln's conduit to African American personhood and as the coauthors' conduit to the theme of race in the novel, which runs not through the mass experience of slave suffering but through the strivings of an imagined black middle class.[32] Slaves and slavery seldom, if ever, appear in this alternate-history trilogy; emancipation is not a question of righting centuries of wrong (nor of facing the inevitable wrath of a just God, as both Lincoln and Jefferson feared) but rather of getting out of the way of enlightened self-determination, which the characters in the Bartlett family embody.

The Gingrich-Forstchen Civil War novels are harbingers of sesquicentennial remembering because they serve as examples of the ways contemporary or postmodern memory (of the Civil War) accepts alternate shapes of the past to enable preferred ways of thinking about the present. There are no racists in the "memory" invoked in *Never Call Retreat*. Slaveholders are all but invisible; black characters appear from time to time as "servants" but not as slaves. The family of free black Bartletts, introduced in *Grant Comes East*, carries, almost exclusively, the theme of race transformed into middle-class striving, and because they are already "free" blacks, they do not stand in need of legal emancipation. The grandfather, Lincoln's majordomo, has a son ("Jim") who is a sergeant major in the Union army (in a segregated unit), and his son, the third generation of Bartletts, is a boy who goes to the front with his father to see his freedom in the making. Just as the counterfactual battle for Washington is heating up, an Irish American colonel tells his black troops that if they hold the line against Confederate assaults, they will earn their liberty and, if victorious, become white Americans as the Irish themselves had through military sacrifice:

> "Sergeant Major, you know there was no love lost between us Irish and you colored."

"I know that, sir."

"Both fighting for the same jobs, both treated as trash. This war is changing that forever."

"I hope so, sir."

"I know so. This day is your day to win what we Irish won at Fredericksburg." (405)[33]

The Bartlett boy is killed in the climactic battle to defend Washington from Confederate invasion.[34]

The Civil War did change race relations in the United States, but political change had to be added to what African American soldiers achieved on the battlefield, and by the time of the semi-centennial the battlefield sacrifices of the Colored Troops were largely forgotten. Abolitionists, black or white, do not appear in the Gingrich-Forstchen revision of the Civil War; readers can indulge in the temporary fantasy (a counterfactual present to accompany the counterfactual past) that civil rights activism (then or later) did not have to happen, that the United States (coexisting with an independent CSA) would have worked out its racial dilemma through the efforts of a black middle class rather than through the emancipation of all those locked in slavery.

Even Gingrich and Forstchen, however, are not completely sure such a miracle can be imagined. As much as the black Bartletts shift the race question from its historical genesis in white supremacy to the empowerment of an incipient black middle class (from Jim Crow to Jim Barlett), they are not the sole portal through which the coauthors strive to rethink American racial politics. Also in *Grant Comes East* is the character John Miller, a free black millworker who escapes Baltimore in the advent of Confederate occupation and enlists in the Union army. Miller's vision of citizenship is more ambiguous than the one touted by the Irish colonel to Sergeant Major Bartlett and his doomed son. As Miller leaves Philadelphia aboard a train loaded with black Union soldiers bound for the front, he sees this:

> The people who were along the tracks had looked upon him and his comrades with amazement. Here was a colored division going to war. Where in the past he had learned to stand detached, head lowered, as if he was not really a man, now he stood looking them in the eye, and many of them waved, some shouting blessings, a woman in a village in western New Jersey passing up a basket of fresh-baked bread. Perhaps Frederick Douglass was right. (364–65)[35]

But Miller's moment of hope that he has finally seized "the rights of citizenship" (365) is soon deflated when he realizes that America will not be his land in his lifetime, and only maybe will the promise be fulfilled for his daughters and grand-children—who would have been, in a simulated lifespan, African Americans whose lives had been lived under Jim Crow and who might have survived to see the fiftieth anniversary of the Civil War when *The Birth of a Nation* and its caricatures summed up much of American thinking on race. Of such feints and retreats are the politics of the counterfactual history made. It is easy enough to imagine a shift of tactics here or there that would bring about a different outcome to a single battle; it is more difficult to imagine a human nature better than the one we know we possess.

The counterfactual occupation of Baltimore by Confederate forces in the summer of 1863 becomes Robert E. Lee's crucible of racial conversion too. Gingrich and Forstchen use counterfactual history to initiate the transformation of Lee from warrior to politician and thereby transform his mythic stature as a warrior into a mythic stature as savior-politician. As escaped slaves and free blacks evacuate the city, for example, J. E. B. Stuart hastily swears an oath to round them all up, allowing the wiser Lee to identify a problem: "General Stuart, just how in God's name will you tell the difference [between free blacks and escaping slaves]?" Lee "rages" in response to the general's inadequate answer, and Stuart, embarrassed, backs down (*Grant* 197). Jefferson Davis, who also wants to return all the "contrabands" to Virginia, requires subtler political massaging, but Lee manages to quell his commander-in-chief's more virulent racism (213). The point is that the reimagined Lee sees beyond the battlefield to the managing of peace in a postwar America that (perhaps in a way even Gingrich and Forstchen do not clearly foresee) will be urban, cosmopolitan, and contemporary.

Converting Lee from cavalier to a politician of moderation is a heavy burden on the plot of *Grant Comes East*. Rather than reinvent Lee's entire biography, Gingrich and Forstchen dramatize the formation of Lee's pragmatic conscience at an imaginary dinner, in the midst of the Baltimore occupation, attended by Lee, Confederate secretary of state Judah Benjamin, and an influential local rabbi, Samuel Rothenberg, Benjamin's confidant and an aficionado of Edgar Allan Poe's work (*Grant* 219–20). Rabbi Rothenberg, host of the dinner, immediately communicates with Lee on a first-name basis. He tells the Confederate general that Lincoln has stolen the race issue and that Lee is the only southern leader capable of getting it back. Lee explains that politics is not his métier; he is a soldier. Rabbi Rothenberg, seeing through Lee's modesty and speaking metatextually for the genre of the counterfactual, exposes the structural principle of the entire effort to re-remember the Civil War in the present: "General Lee . . . if ever there has been a political war in history, it is this one. It is the heart and soul of this conflict" (*Grant* 226). The Civil War, as Gingrich and Forstchen (and many other authors of counterfactual histories as well) simulate it, is a political war—a war to replace the actual politics of secession, war, and "redemption" from Reconstruction (all implicated in a national American culture of white supremacy) with a reimagined "politics" that cleanses "southernization" in U.S. politics of its underlying racism before the "rebel germ" even appears and represents it as a wise, seasoned conservative pragmatism that would have gotten (and still might get) the nation to a guiltless conscience. In other words, alternate history attempts to alter what we remember about the past to create a plausible (simulated) ground for a counterfactual present in which certain political positions can be held without the burden of knowing that they have already failed.

In *Never Call Retreat*, Gingrich and Forstchen conclude their counterfactual Civil War with a negotiated peace settlement, not the unconditional surrender of Appomattox. Lee and Grant do not fight on through the grueling Virginia campaign of history, nor does Sherman march through Georgia and the Carolinas. Lee and Grant agree on terms by the end of August 1863. Lee's Maryland campaign, at moments, looks as if it might succeed, but the Union's superior numbers ultimately wear down the Army of Northern Virginia. In an elaborate endgame, Lee and Grant meet in Frederick, Maryland, to discuss terms. Grant is honorable and generous, willing to stop well short of unconditional surrender if Lee will agree to disarm. The two professional soldiers see war and postwar in very similar terms, and their part in the scene of surrender is quickly concluded.

Gingrich and Forstchen, countering in part the majority of previous portraits of Lee, do not allow him to exit history into legend; they make sure he leaves for future political battles in Richmond with Jefferson Davis and his right-wing faction in the Confederate Congress. To carry on negotiations to end the war, Gingrich and Forstchen choose Elihu Washburne, an Illinois congressman and confidant of Lincoln, whom the co-authors pluck from the House of Representatives, where he was the ultimate insider, and imagine as the successor to Edwin Stanton as secretary of war. Washburne and Judah P. Benjamin, the Confederate secretary of state, take over to plan the peace. When one of the revisionist authors (Gingrich) is a politician, the end of the war cannot be left solely to the soldiers.[36] Washburne, carrying dispatches from Lincoln, insists that Benjamin persuade the Confederate government in Richmond to pledge allegiance to the Constitution, disband all Confederate armies, and cease all firing—not just on the Virginia front but in the West as well. Furthermore, the South is to recognize the Emancipation Proclamation by acts in each of the legislatures of the seceding states. In return, Lincoln promises to put a southerner on the ticket as his vice president in the election of 1864 and through the Homestead Act promises to set aside settlement land in the West for the freed slaves. Benjamin is intrigued. Washburne, a veteran dealmaker, figured he would be. Generals might move regiments and brigades on the field of battle, but the strategy that counts is in the political deal.

Elihu leaned forward and stared straight at Judah.

"Sir, if we do not agree to this point, I fear that what helped to cause this war, the issue of slavery and race, will continue to fester within us for the next hundred years. I do not wish to sound overly sentimental or patriotic, but the Declaration did declare that all men are created equal. I want to believe that the four of us, sitting here, can help that to come true."

Judah sighed.

"And yet human nature being what it is, I hope your dream is true, Elihu. I have a friend in Baltimore, a rabbi, who shared basically the same thoughts with me just a few weeks past. Yes, he is right, and so are you. As a Jew I should be more sensitive to that than most. The history of my people is replete with persecutions, and I fear in times to come it will happen again, perhaps even worse than what was endured before." (586)

Although history testifies that the states of the Confederacy did not, except under duress, acknowledge that all men are created equal, it is understandable to indulge in a counterfactual scenario that airbrushes such flaws. Assuming that, in the domain of alternate history, individual states in the South had adopted emancipation, then one is more easily persuaded that subsequent forms of federal regulation were arbitrary and unnecessary. Unwritten but implied in the Gingrich-Forstchen simulation of history, the actual history of civil rights legislation running through the Thirteenth, Fourteenth, and Fifteenth Amendments up to the Civil Rights and Voting Rights Acts of the 1960s and affirmative action would never have occurred, and the constituencies thus attached to those causes would never have formed on the political landscape. In the political past summoned to "memory" by most counterfactual histories of the Civil War, there are no circumstances that make activism for civil rights necessary. The promises made by the federal government after Appomattox were never broken because they were never made in the (alternate) first place. We enjoy a simpler political past and cleaner present because our Civil War ended not in surrender but in a truce. This might seem like a small distinction, but an imagined truce bequeaths to us a moderately rather than totally triumphant Union and a different national temperament.

In the final chapter of *Never Call Retreat*, two definitive events anoint the alternate union: Lincoln begins to deliver his "Frederick" Address (in the counterfactual past Frederick, Maryland, not Gettysburg, Pennsylvania, is the site of the definitive battle), and Lee speaks to the Confederate Congress in Richmond, defying Jefferson Davis's orders to continue the fighting and thereby violate the truce the honorable and moderate Lee had pledged to Grant. The simulation gives us two separate yet equal political pasts because it gives us two nations (the one we actually have, underwritten by Lincoln's rhetoric, and one we can imagine with counterfactual help, in which the South evolved out of racial binarism and white supremacy without the intervention of a central government): civil war without a loser.

Where Gingrich and Forstchen see the Civil War without a losing side, E. L. Doctorow sees a more sinister era come into being, one that includes even more sweeping, dark changes than those trailing in the wake of our racial politics—one in which our Civil War, just in taking place, made us all losers. As Doctorow sees the Civil War in his novel *The March* (2005), there was enough loss in the war to seep into the rest of U.S. history and curdle it with modernity.[37] Like the Gingrich-Forstchen alternate histories of the Civil War, Doctorow projects his present into the past. Unlike the Gingrich-Forstchen work, however, Doctorow does not rearrange history to imagine how much more favorable to present myth it might be but rather to compel us to see that our Homeric period in the past was but an undetected prelude to our dystopian present.

The plot of *The March* is strung along the historical timeline of Sherman's march from Georgia through the Carolinas in late 1864 and the first half of 1865, beginning with the occupation of Atlanta and concluding with the surrender of the Confederate army under Joe Johnston in North Carolina. Most counterfactuals truncate the Civil War so that this endgame never takes place. The themes of Doctorow's novel circulate through many of the characters swept into the march. General William T. Sherman, for obvious reasons, is one of the poles of the novel's contemplations. Doctorow tends to use characters as symptoms of large flows of ominous change in the culture of the United States, and Sherman is useful as an agent, albeit largely unwitting, of the modern temperament he prophetically embodies. Sherman's march is the central metaphor for a loosely directed, omnivorously consuming, amoeba-like nation that grows with no plan beyond the slaking of its own hungers. Early in the novel, in a scene set in Milledgeville, Georgia, Emily Thompson, daughter of a southern, secessionist judge, likens advance units of Sherman's army to an "infestation" and a "swarm" (26). The insect metaphor might be seen as predictable, lodged as it is in the imagination of a character conceived as a southern loyalist, but there is no countering metaphor on the Union side save the bloodless exactitude of science—no imagined alternative to the present we inhabit. If we were using Robert Penn Warren's terms, there would be no Treasury of Virtue funding Union actions in the war and no Great Alibi either.

Emily Thompson sees the swarming victory of modernity. After her father dies, she temporarily succumbs to the Svengali-like powers of Wrede Sartorious, a surgeon attached to Sherman's army.[38] Initially, Emily thinks Sartorious is a brilliant doctor overwhelmed by the number and severity of battlefield wounds. Searching for medical help for her father in Union-occupied Milledgeville, Emily finds a field hospital and this: "On the ground outside the open barn doors was something from which she couldn't in time avert her eyes. She didn't want to believe she was looking at a slimed heap of severed human arms and legs" (29). Walt Whitman had seen similar mounds of amputated human limbs and reported them in *Specimen Days* (1882). Whitman's experience of the wounded did not diminish his faith in the body, and Emily seems, at first sight of Sartorious, the surgeon who is producing all of the severed parts, to think of him as heroic: "He was a short, neatly put-together man who seemed inviolate in the carnage around him. He wore a rubber apron over his tunic. A bloodied saw was in his hand. He had thick eyebrows, and the eyes that had peered from under them were a pale blue. It seemed to her they were filled with an anguish that reflected her own" (29). But Emily is mistaken; Sartorious's eyes are not full of anguish but monomania. Medical service on the battlefield is not a mission of mercy for Sartorious but the opportunity for nonstop and unmonitored medical research. He can foresee the breakthroughs, the emblems of modern progress: "We will have found botanical molds to reverse infection. We will replace lost blood. We will photograph through the body to the bones. And so on" (59). Sartorious's drive to reduce the human body to its mechanical parts and processes denudes him of humanity. When Emily and Sartorious finally make love, to her horror she finds his amorous technic quite robotic; he nicks her hymen with a surgical tool before intercourse. "And at the moment of his crisis," Doctorow continues, "she made the mistake of opening her eyes, and in the light of the hearth fire his face was hideous, contorted by a stunned and mindless expression, the eyes frozen in a blind stare that seemed to her an agony of perception as if into a godless universe" (143). She ultimately concludes that for all the "progress of science" summed up in Sartorious, he is "a magus bent on tampering with the created universe" (190).[39] Emily flees her demon lover and returns to Milledgeville to "wait there for that army of which this army on the march is just fanfare" (210).

Herein lies the encompassing allegory of *The March*, and the powerful attrition of the war in the contemporary era: the disordered "progress" of modern life lived *en masse* is figured by Doctorow's version of the March to the Sea as it accumulates freed slaves, a pair of shape-shifting Confederate deserters, southern white refugees, a London war correspondent, and an assortment of white Union soldiers and officers—some of whom are introduced in the narrative and willy-nilly killed. Modernity sweeps us forward to changes we can neither comprehend nor shape, but we remain addicted to the next step.

Although we call this change progress, there is no sign or guarantee that it makes us better human beings or our civilization more humane. Historian James Cobb shared the same theme when he observed that, in the identity processes of North and South, "[t]he North also represented the combined forces of an intrusive, unsettling, faith-and-tradition-shaking modernity" opposed to the traditionalism of the South (5). In Doctorow's dark vision, however, there is no relief in thinking of the South as an alternative.

Sherman comes to the realization of what he and his march represent only after the swarm has spread far beyond his control. He did not know it in Columbia, South Carolina, as the city burned down to its masonry chimneys after a Union bacchanal. Accepting Joe Johnston's surrender in North Carolina, Sherman shivers with a dread of modernity he still cannot actually name as such: "Suddenly, Sherman felt a great sympathy for his enemy [Gen. Johnston], this wily old bird with the small bright eyes and a nose like a grosbeak's. There was a bond of recognition here, they were of the same school. They were both damned fine soldiers. He felt more trusting of this general, an enemy, than he was of his superiors in Washington—Stanton, Andrew Johnson the presumed new president, the whole cabal of Washington politicians who aroused in him, at best, a wariness of their intentions" (347). What lies at the termination of *The March* / the march is not a new nation presided over by "the better angels of our nature" but the modern nation-state driven by capital flows, political interests, and the amoral compulsions of power, a nation that will, as Doctorow is writing *The March* in the early years of the twenty-first century, take retribution for the attacks of 9/11 into wars of choice in Iraq and Afghanistan.[40]

Insofar as *The March*, like the Gingrich-Forstchen trilogy, calls on its readers to remember the Civil War, it asks us to think of the war as a harbinger of changes and forces we cannot (now or ever) have known otherwise. Implied in other counterfactual histories of the war is the argument that, had the ending come not in total surrender by the South but in a negotiated truce that preserved some of the seceding states' control over their political futures, the nation of rememberers in the present day would have been spared much of the civil rights turmoil that followed the failure of Reconstruction, and the ongoing political battles over the meaning of federalism would have been settled long before New Deal programs came forth from a central government "cabal of Washington politicians" and made Americans think that *laissez faire* was not the only way to conduct the people's business. Not so in *The March*.

Doctorow's argument is not so far different from the conservative counterfactual in one respect: the present (modernity) is not a condition we might have chosen, but it is commensurate to the human race's potential for losing Faustian bargains. The difference lies in Doctorow's melancholic realization that history is not reversible, even by acts of the imagination. *The March* seems to assert that the past was a whole lot like the present and therefore no refuge from the sorrows of now. It is clear, for example, that the author of *The March* in the twenty-first century, closing in on 150 years after the Civil War, knows that the thousands of freed black slaves who follow in Sherman's wake are not going to find the justice our national rhetoric promises. To emphasize the point, Doctorow dramatizes the visit of Secretary of War Stanton to Sherman in Savannah with the news that in addition to his military duties Sherman will have to implement the Emancipation Proclamation in the southern territory liberated by his army. "Governance," Sherman fumes, is not war (116). Field Order No. 15, confiscating tens of thousands of acres of land in the path of his march and redistributing it in forty-acre allotments to freed slaves, was neither Sherman's anticipation of human reconstruction nor just an expedient to jettison a swelling African American population that was hindering his ability to move his army. It was in Doctorow's depiction an annoyance and afterthought:

> "Your pen, Major [Teack, Sherman's aide]. Get this down. Field Order whatever it is.
>
> It would be Number 15, sir. . . .
>
> I am no abolitionist, Sherman thought. But with this enticement I both shut up Edwin Stanton and disengage the niggers, who will stay here to plant their forty acres, and God help them." (120)

Sherman's meager good wishes to the freedmen were, historically, as futile as they sound in fiction; Field Order No. 15 was rescinded by Andrew Johnson less than a year later.

As *The March* ends, it is, surprisingly, Sherman himself who delivers the valediction, written by Doctorow no doubt in the midst of another American war in the twenty-first century—a war about which Doctorow was not shy in his opinions:

> Though this march is done, and well accomplished, I think of it now, God help me, with longing—not for its blood and death but for the bestowal of meaning to the very ground trod upon, how it made every field and swamp and river and road into something of moral consequence, whereas now, as the march dissolves so does the meaning, the army strewing itself into the isolated intentions of diffuse private life, and the terrain thereby left blank and also diffuse, and ineffable, a thing once again, and victoriously, without reason, and whether diurnally lit and darkened, or sere or fruitful, or raging or calm, completely insensible and without any purpose of its own.
>
> And why is Grant so solemn today upon our great achieve-

ment, except he knows this unmeaning inhuman planet will need our warring imprint to give it value, and that our civil war, the devastating manufacture of the bones of our sons, is but a war after a war, a war before a war. (358–59)

Doctorow's Sherman seems to see, from the perspective of the "well accomplished" event, that it is in fact the event, not the commemoration, that bestows meaning. So for Sherman and *The March*, "the isolated intentions of diffuse private life" can be unified in "moral consequence" only by "a war after a war, a war before a war." Nothing is said about rituals of commemoration: anniversaries, centennials of any multiple of 50 or 100 or 150. So it must have seemed to Doctorow in the years before the publication of *The March*, the years of the post-9/11 wars of the twenty-first century, that the Sherman temperament ("this unmeaning inhuman planet will need our warring imprint to give it value") had become the prevailing temperament of the modern, nationalistic, corporate state. We are, in Doctorow's view it seems, smaller than our history, forever mistaking its meaning, forever hiding from ourselves in the rituals of public memory. It is really the blood and destruction we miss; we commemorate past wars with new ones.

Lest I close on this note of bottomless dystopia, let's return to *Captain Confederacy II* and one of the transformations I deliberately withheld in my earlier plot summary. Kate has become the new Captain Confederacy, and she is pregnant: a black woman, in red, white, and blue maternity clothes with a swatch of the battle flag stretched snug across her shoulders. The father of her child is the former Captain Confederacy, now known as Kid Dixie. Perhaps the ease of transformations from male to female, from white to African American, are symptomatic of the proliferating hybrid identities of our postmodern era, and the child of Captain Confederacy's womb will be the hybrid to abolish race distinction once for all—and "the struggle for civil rights" along with it. The child of the new Confederacy was (as Shetterly's story would have it) possibly conceived in a dream. But it is a familiar dream, one we have had before as a nightmare. Will what was once anathema, the romance of mixed blood, become the language in which we remember the Civil War?

Notes

❦

Preface

1. What to call the anniversaries is a potential cause of confusion. Most are familiar with "centennial," but less so with its two relatives. I have used identifiers interchangeably: semicentennial and 50th anniversary, centennial and 100th anniversary, and sesquicentennial and 150th anniversary.

2. Pierre Nora, "Between Memory and History: *Les Lieux de Mémoire*," *Representations* 26 (Spring 1989): 7–24.

3. W. Fitzhugh Brundage, *Where These Memories Grow: History, Memory, and Southern Identity* (Chapel Hill: University of North Carolina Press, 2000).

4. As if to assert that the past is never dead but rather is intellectual property, the Faulkner Foundation of Oxford, Mississippi, has recently sued SONY Pictures over what the Foundation alleges is a copyright infringement: the lead character in Woody Allen's film *Midnight in Paris* (2011) not only misquotes the line but does so without permission.

5. David W. Blight, *Race and Reunion: The Civil War in American Memory* (Cambridge, Mass.: Belknap Press, 2001); *American Oracle: The Civil War in the Civil Rights Era* (Cambridge, Mass.: Belknap Press, 2011).

Chapter 1. Remembering the Civil War in the Era of Race Suicide

1. "Love and Marriage," lyrics by Sammy Cahn; music Jimmy Van Heusen. Recorded by Frank Sinatra, Capitol Records, 1955.

2. Blood transfusions had been attempted for years, usually with fatal results for the recipients, but blood types were not known until 1901 when Dr. Karl Landsteiner established the first three human blood

groups, and it was not until six years later, in 1907, that transfusions using typed and cross-matched blood were successfully performed.

3. Tom Buchanan has author and title confused, but Fitzgerald refers to Lothrop Stoddard, *The Rising Tide of Color against White World-Supremacy* (New York: Charles Scribner's Sons, 1922).

4. F. Scott Fitzgerald, *The Great Gatsby* (New York: Charles Scribner's Sons, 1925). Edmund Morris, in his *Theodore Rex* (New York: Modern Library, 2002), describes his subject similarly, save for the sinister connotations Fitzgerald uses: "His tanned skin stretched over his jutting jaw. His teeth gleamed through thick, half-parted lips. His neck, too squat for a standing collar, merged with weight-lifter shoulders, sloping two full inches to the tip of his biceps, and his chest pushed apart the lapels of his frock coat. He tugged at his watch chain with short, nervous fingers, shifting his small, square-toed shoes. Here, palpably, was a man of expansive force" (17).

5. Theodore Roosevelt, "On American Motherhood," speech given on March 13, 1905, www.nationalcenter.org/TRooseveltMotherhood .html (accessed June 8, 2012). Edmund Morris writes in *Theodore Rex* that during a stop in "Iowa's fecund fields" in 1903, President Roosevelt was cheered by "women in faded Mother Hubbard gowns . . . their arms bursting with progeny" under a banner that proclaimed: "NO 'RACE SUICIDE' HERE, TEDDY!" (224).

6. Thomas G. Dyer, *Theodore Roosevelt and The Idea of Race* (Baton Rouge: Louisiana State University Press, 1992), 24–25; Theodore Roosevelt, "The Expansion of White Races" address at the Celebration of the Diamond Jubilee of the African Methodist Episcopal Church in Washington, D.C., June 18, 1909, www.theodore-roosevelt.com/images /research/speeches/trwhiteraces.pdf (accessed June 8, 2012).

7. Robert Grant, *Unleavened Bread* (New York: Charles Scribner's Sons, 1900).

8. David Starr Jordan and Harvey Ernest Jordan, *War's Aftermath: A Preliminary Study of the Eugenics of War* (Boston: Houghton Mifflin, 1914).

9. An example of the transformation of the theme of race or blood into romance and sex springs from Roosevelt's dinner with Booker T. Washington at the White House in October 1901. The dinner was not "advanced" by the Roosevelt administration, nor was news of it disseminated until the daily schedule was released to the press well after the dinner had ended. Southern newspapers ratcheted the theme up

from cordial dinner to sexual outrage. Edmund Morris, in *Theodore Rex*, reports: "Some of the more sensational sheets expressed sexual disgust at the idea of Edith Roosevelt [the President's wife] and Washington touching thighs, so to speak, under the table" (55).

10. As an example of the powerful contradictoriness inherent in race and blood thinking, consider that David Starr Jordan, in *The Blood of the Nation: A Study of the Decay of Races through the Survival of the Unfit* (Boston: American Unitarian Association, 1916), wrote: "We know that the actual blood in the actual veins plays no part in heredity, that the transfusion of blood means no more than the transposition of food, and that the physical basis of the phenomenon of inheritance is found in the structure of the germ cell and its contained germ-plasm" (8–9). Yet in *War's Aftermath* he describes the "blood" of the southern dead with the rhetoric of "knightly spirit," "superior males," and "martyrs" (21, 47, 78). So also does his cowriter Harvey Ernest Jordan (no relation) in "The Biological Status and Social Worth of the Mulatto," *Popular Science* (June 1913): 573–82. The latter Jordan finds the same soul in the white and the "hybrid" and yet sees the "social worth" of the mulatto as breeding stock only, toward a racial end, not an end in itself: "The mulatto is the leaven with which to lift the negro race. He serves as our best lever for negro elevation. The mulatto does not feel the instinctive mental nausea to negro mating. He might even be made to feel a sacred mission in this regard. The negro aspires to be mulatto. The mulatto to be white" (580–81).

11. It would be interesting to bring Whitman back, if only to have him read novels such as Geraldine Brooks's *March* or E. L. Doctorow's *The March*, both of which feature prominently and repeatedly bloody scenes in military field hospitals. See the third essay in this collection.

12. Griffith also drew from Dixon's earlier novel, *The Leopard's Spots* (1902).

13. Woodrow Wilson and Edward S. Corwin, *Epochs of American History: Division and Reunion,* rev. ed. (New York: Longmans, Green, 1921).

14. Theodore Roosevelt, "The Expansion of the White Races," 1, 2.

15. Quoted in David W. Blight, *Race and Reunion: The Civil War in American Memory* (Cambridge, Mass.: Belknap Press, 2001), 11.

16. See Blight and also Drew Gilpin Faust, *The Republic of Suffering: Death and the American Civil War* (New York: Alfred A. Knopf, 2008).

17. Dixon and Wilson were classmates at Princeton, and Griffith used excerpts from Wilson's histories on title cards in his film.

18. A precursor novel to Dixon's is Thomas Nelson Page, *Red Rock: A Chronicle of Reconstruction* (New York: Charles Scribner's Sons, 1898). Courtship and marriage plots crisscross the novel and eventually cinch its climax. Although Page steers away from outright rape, he does hint at its possibility in a scene involving a white woman and a mulatto male character (292).

19. Edward Sheldon, *"The Nigger": An American Play in Three Acts* (New York: Macmillan Company, 1915). The film adaptation, retitled *The Governor*, was released in March 1915, a month after *The Birth of a Nation* opened in Los Angeles.

20. "Fighting Race Calumny," *The Crisis* (May 1915): 40–42; "Photo Plays and Branches," *The Crisis* (September 1915): 245. See also Blight, *Race and Reunion*, 395–97.

21. The flaming stereotypes in the film and novel are not that distantly removed from more genteel and scholarly versions of themselves. Take, for one example, the Pulitzer Prize–winning book by Paul H. Buck, *The Road to Reunion, 1865–1900*, published in 1937—between *Gone with the Wind* the novel (1936) and the film (1939). *The Road to Reunion* grew out of Harvard University's History Department, as Buck's dissertation, and it is dedicated to Arthur Meier Schlesinger, one of the strongest beacons of progressive U.S. history in the twentieth century. Still, Buck treads perilously close to the vein of stereotype Dixon and Griffith mined two decades earlier. In Buck's view, "the not inhumane institution of slavery both made and destroyed the hope of Southern nationalism" (ix). And the repressive measures enacted by Jim Crow regimes after the termination of Reconstruction in 1877 (literacy tests for voting, limitations to civil and legal rights) were seen by Buck as forms of "discipline" rather than terror (289). Images broadcast by Dixon and Griffith might certainly have been more incendiary—several local jurisdictions, agreeing with the NAACP, banned showings of *The Birth of a Nation* for fear of inciting audiences (to what actions is not specified)—but Buck's award-winning work was merely more genteel. When Buck writes, "Best of all, the discipline [of Jim Crow] prevented the Negro from slipping into semi-barbarism, gave him a job and a permanent place in Southern life, and permitted a slow but definite progress for the race as a whole" (290), he places Dixon's images of black and mulatto rapists into a coded script (290). And when he titles his chapter

"The Negro Problem Always Ye Have With You," his patronizing racism is different in virulence, but not in kind.

22. Economizing on actors in *The Birth of a Nation*, and at the same time intensifying the theme of blood relationships in the story, Griffith converted the character of Marion Lenoir into Ben Cameron's youngest sister. The character of Mrs. Lenoir was deleted. This alteration of course brings rape and revenge into Cameron's immediate family rather than his communal one.

Chapter 2. The Last Living Memory

1. "Gettysburg Celebration to Be Attended by 3,500 Vets," *Daily Times* (Beaver County, Pa.) June 11, 1938, http://news.google.com/news papers?id=7qoiAAAAIBAJ&sjid=sK8FAAAAIBAJ&pg=3518,3595922 &dq=1938+roosevelt+gettysburg&hl=en (accessed April 10, 2013).

2. William Lundy (1848–1957), John Salling (1848–1959), and Walter Williams (c. 1842–1959).

3. *St. Petersburg Times*, August 3, 1956, 1 (photo), 2 (Eisenhower).

4. David W. Blight, *American Oracle: The Civil War in the Civil Rights Era* (Cambridge, Mass: Belknap Press, 2011), 110, 106.

5. Bruce Catton, "Muffled Roll for the Grand Army," *Life*, August 20, 1956, 19–24.

6. Robert Penn Warren, *The Legacy of the Civil War* (1961; reprint, Lincoln: University of Nebraska Press, 1998), 78.

7. Nor does Catton weave into his eulogy for Woolson and his era the historical fact of the lynchings of three African American men, workers for an itinerant circus in Duluth in June 1920. The men had been falsely accused of raping a white woman. Bob Dylan, who was born Robert Zimmerman in Duluth in 1941, commemorated the lynchings in his song "Desolation Row" (1965).

8. For a detailed discussion of the problems of the Centennial Commission, see Robert J. Cook, *Troubled Commemoration: The American Civil War Centennial, 1961–1965* (Baton Rouge: LSU Press, 2007).

9. David O. Selznick to Kay Brown, quoted in David Thomson, *Showman: The Life of David O. Selznick* (New York: Alfred A. Knopf, 1992), 320–21.

10. Following advice and standard Hollywood thinking that "by mid-1942, *Gone With the Wind* had had its run," Selznick sold his share to partners in his production company (Thomson 379–80). Even

by 1961 *Gone with the Wind* was clearly on its way to becoming the mother lode.

11. See Laura McCarty, "Civil War Centennial," *New Georgia Encyclopedia*, September 14, 2010, http://www.georgiaencyclopedia.org /nge/ArticlePrintable.jsp?id=h-3752 (accessed April 10, 2013).

12. Not even Albert Woolson, the actual Civil War veteran, was immune to fictionalizing his memory. In an interview conducted in 1954, when he was 107, Woolson told interviewers that he had seen John Wilkes Booth act and described the meeting of Grant and Lee at Appomattox as if he had been an eyewitness. See "Listen to a 1954 Interview with the Last Surviving Union Civil War Vet," *New Tribune Attic*, March 1, 2011, http://attic.areavoices.com/2011/03/01/listen-to-a-1954-interview-with -the-last-surviving-union-civil-war-vet/ (accessed April 10, 2013).

13. Flannery O'Connor, *The Complete Stories* (New York: Farrar Straus & Giroux, 1971), 135.

14. See "Last Survivor of the Civil War," *Life*, May 11, 1959, 48–50.

15. Quoted in Brad Gooch, *Flannery: A Life of Flannery O'Connor* (New York: Little Brown, 2009), 68.

16. L. Jesse Lemisch, "Who Won the Civil War Anyway?" *The Nation* 192, no. 4 (1961): 300–302, quote on 300. For more about the author, see the page devoted to him on the website Discover the Networks: A Guide to the Political Left, http://www.discoverthenetworks .org/individualProfile.asp?indid=1994.

17. "Winning" the centennial could be accomplished in passive ways. *The Americans*, a weekly television series broadcast on NBC from January to May 1961, followed the lives of two brothers from a Virginia family who fought on opposite sides in the war. Slavery was not mentioned in any of the seventeen episodes, and the series title, *The Americans*, solidified what David Blight termed "the resubjugation" of the slaves by not including them in that category.

18. Edmund Wilson, *Patriotic Gore* (New York: Oxford University Press, 1962). For an extended discussion of Wilson and *Patriotic Gore*, see David W. Blight, *American Oracle*.

19. The song "Abraham, Martin and John," written by Dick Holler in 1968, remembers three assassinated American leaders: Abraham Lincoln, Martin Luther King Jr., and John F. Kennedy.

20. Robert Penn Warren, "A Mark Deep on a Nation's Soul," *Life*, March 17, 1961, 82–88. Random House published a longer and fuller version as *The Legacy of the Civil War* later in 1961. Because the ver-

sions are different and I quote from both, excerpts from the *Life* text are identified by "L" and the Random House text by "RH." Warren's essay was the sixth and final installment of a series on the Civil War published by *Life* in the early months of the centennial year. It was preceded by Bruce Catton, "Gallant Men in Deeds of Glory," *Life*, January 6, 1961, 48–50, 63–64, 66–70; a gallery of paintings of Civil War battles by *Life* artists, "Now History, the Battles," January 20, 1961, 53–83; Bell Irvin Wiley, "The Soldier's Life," February 3, 1961, 64–66, 71–74, 77; Lt. Gen. James M. Gavin, "Great Advances That Changed War," February 17, 1961, 67–70, 76, 79–82; Margaret Leech, "Gaiety and Dread on the Home Front," March 3, 1961, 68–72, 78, 80, 83, 86, 89.

21. For an indication of this "different Civil War memory," see David Blight's introduction to *American Oracle*, in which he reminds us of the Civil War imagery in Martin Luther King Jr.'s "I Have a Dream" address from August 28, 1963.

22. Not surprisingly, "the ad-man's nauseating surrogate for family sense and community in the word *togetherness*" does not appear in the *Life* text—financed as it was by advertising agency images of white families happily consuming national brands of food, clothing, transportation, and insurance.

23. MacKinlay Kantor, *If The South Had Won the Civil War* (New York: Forge Books, 2001). Originally published in *Look*, November 22, 1960, 29–62.

24. See Scott Romine, *The Real South: Southern Narrative in an Age of Cultural Reproduction* (Baton Rouge: LSU Press, 2008).

25. Robert Penn Warren, *Wilderness: A Tale of the Civil War* (New York: Random House, 1961). For a summary of critical reception, see Joseph Blotner, *Robert Penn Warren: A Biography* (New York: Random House, 1997), 346–49.

26. Blotner, *Robert Penn Warren* (4, 416), assesses the impact of Warren's father on his work.

27. *Major Dundee,* directed by Sam Peckinpah (Columbia Pictures, 1965).

Chapter 3. The Civil War and Its Afterlife

1. Will Shetterly and Vince Stone, *Captain Confederacy* (n.p., 2007); Will Shetterly and Vince Stone, *Captain Confederacy 2* (n.p., 2012).

Shetterly is the plotter and writer; Stone draws. *Captain Confederacy* originally ran in twelve comic book issues published by SteelDragon Press from 1986 to 1988. John M. Ford coplotted and wrote parts of the first series. The second series was published in four issues by Epic Comics (a division of Marvel), 1991–92. Captain Confederacy dies, then returns to life by means of a secret drug. The plot explanations are too arcane to summarize; the important thing is that Captain Confederacy is reborn.

2. This darker premise—that slavery might have survived—is the one taken up by Kevin Wilmott in his "mockumentary" film *CSA: The Confederate States of America* (IFC Films, 2004).

3. James C. Cobb, *Away Down South: A History of Southern Identity* (New York: Oxford University Press, 2005), 7.

4. William Faulkner, *The Sound and the Fury*, ed. David Minter (New York: W. W. Norton & Co., 1987), 53.

5. Louis D. Rubin Jr. et al., eds., *The History of Southern Literature* (Baton Rouge: Louisiana State University Press, 1985).

6. Taken further, by Scott Romine, into an age of cultural reproduction in which the distinction between a perception of reality and reality itself is difficult or impossible, the issue of identity is cut off from the circumstances of lived experience. See Scott Romine, *The Real South: Southern Narrative in an Age of Cultural Reproduction* (Baton Rouge: Louisiana State University Press, 2008).

7. One of Cobb's influential models, historian David M. Potter, whom Cobb cites in *Away Down South*, had a less conflicted but still perception-based relationship to the South. In the preface to *The South and the Sectional Conflict* (1968) Potter writes that "although I was born in Georgia in 1910, I have always had a feeling that in an indirect, nonsensory way I could remember what was still called 'The War'—as if there had been no other" (v). Potter was of the generation represented in the previous lecture by Robert Penn Warren: white men born in the South around the time of the semicentennial who, during the centennial, worried over the disappearance of living witnesses to the reality of their memory. See David M. Potter, *The South and the Sectional Conflict* (Baton Rouge: Louisiana State University Press, 1968).

8. C. Hugh Holman, "The View from the Regency Hyatt," in *The Roots of Southern Writing* (Athens: University of Georgia Press, 1972), 96–107.

9. W. Fitzhugh Brundage, *Where These Memories Grow: History, Memory, and Southern Identity* (Chapel Hill: UNC Press, 2000), 2.

10. Senator Barack Obama, campaigning for the Democratic nomination for president, in "A More Perfect Union," address delivered March 18, 2008.

11. For a heavy dose of shame and guilt, see Chuck Thompson, *Better Off Without 'Em: A Northern Manifesto for Southern Secession* (New York: Simon & Schuster, 2012).

12. Blight, *Race and Reunion: The Civil War in American Memory* (Cambridge, Mass.: Belknap Press, 2001) and *American Oracle: The Civil War in the Civil Rights Era* (Cambridge, Mass: Belknap Press, 2011).

13. David W. Blight, "150 Years after Fort Sumter, Forces That Gave Rise to the Civil War Still Plague Modern America," *New York Daily News*, April 12, 2011, www.nydailynews.com/opinion/150-years -fort-sumter-forces-gave-rise-civil-war-plague-modern-america-article -1.1151 (accessed April 11, 2013).

14. David Potter corroborates Blight's reading of the immunities accorded the Civil War. For Potter, the Civil War enjoyed "protected status as an American Iliad" (ix).

15. A bill to establish a federal commission was introduced into the U.S. Senate by Senator Jim Webb (D. Va.) in March 2011. It was assigned to a committee and has not been heard of since. See www .govtrack.us/congress/bills/112/s559/text (accessed April 11, 2013). The website www.civilwar.org/150th-anniversary/150-website reports that thirty states have, at least, formed websites if not full-fledged commissions or initiatives. One state, North Carolina, has two: one is called the North Carolina Civil War Sesquicentennial (www.nccivilwar150 .com) and the other the North Carolina War Between the States Sesquicentennial (www.ncwbts150.com) dedicated to exposing so-called Marxist and politically correct corruptions of Civil War memory and history (both sites accessed April 21, 2013). The meaning of the Civil War might be argued in terminology. Chuck Thompson, in *Better Off without 'Em*, reports on the case of a proposed history course at the Citadel to carry the title "Charleston and the War for Southern Independence" (293–94).

16. Rick Hampson, "Across the South, an Enduring Conflict," *USA Today*, February 17, 2011, 1A–2A.

17. *2000 Maniacs*, directed by Herschell Gordon Lewis (Jacqueline Kay Company, 1964).

18. Seth Grahame-Smith, *Abraham Lincoln: Vampire Hunter* (New York: Grand Central Publishing, 2010). The film: *Abraham Lincoln: Vampire Hunter*, directed by D. Timur Bekmambetov (Abraham Productions, 2012).

19. Coleridge wrote: "Seeing him [Kean] act was like reading Shakespeare by flashes of lightning." Samuel Taylor Coleridge, *Table Talk of S. T. Coleridge and "The Rime of the Ancient Mariner"* (London: George Routledge and Sons, 1884), 38. Coleridge's comment is dated April 27, 1823.

20. Robert K. Sutton, "Holding the High Ground: Interpreting the Civil War in National Parks," *George Wright Forum* 25, no. 3 (2008): 53, www.georgewright.org/253sutton.pdf (accessed April 11, 2013).

21. For an example, see the National Park Service document "Civil War to Civil Rights: From Pea Ridge to Central High," www.nps.gov/chsc/forteachers/upload/Civil-War-to-Civil-Rights-Lesson-Plan.pdf (accessed April 11, 2013).

22. Edward L. Ayers, ed. *America's War: Talking about the Civil War and Emancipation on Their 150th Anniversaries* (Washington, D.C.: American Library Association and the National Endowment for the Humanities, 2012). The table of contents is available at the ALA's store webpage for the book, www.alastore.ala.org/detail.aspx?ID=3564. I participated as visiting scholar in one of the ALA/NEH programs at the Brentwood, Tennessee, Library.

23. Adam Goodheart, *1861: The Civil War Awakening* (New York: Alfred A. Knopf, 2011), 357–58.

24. Less temperate than Goodheart is Chuck Thompson, *Better Off without 'Em: A Northern Manifesto for Southern Secession*.

25. David Bromwich, "The Rebel Germ," *New York Review of Books*, November 25, 2010, 4–8.

26. Alexander Stephens, "'Cornerstone' Speech," *America's War*, 53.

27. Another example appears in Paul Krugman, "Abraham Lincoln, Inflationist," *New York Times*, February 11, 2011, A25. Krugman is critical of conservative economic theories, and uses the term "neo-secessionism" to caricature them.

28. Tony Horwitz, *Confederates in the Attic: Dispatches from the Unfinished Civil War* (New York: Vintage, 1999).

29. Gingrich and Forstchen, *Gettysburg* (New York: St. Martin's,

2003), *Grant Comes East* (New York: Thomas Dunne, 2004), and *Never Call Retreat* (New York: Thomas Dunne, 2005). Newt Gingrich solo or with Robert Forstchen and other coauthors has published more than twenty books. See Andrew Ferguson, "What Does Newt Know?," *New York Times Magazine,* July 3, 2011, 18–21, 36. Ferguson seems not to be interested in Gingrich's Civil War trilogy, limiting comments on these books to two paragraphs on the final page of his essay. Many will notice that Gingrich and Forstchen use the title of the third volume of Bruce Catton's *Centennial History of the Civil War, Never Call Retreat* (New York: Doubleday, 1965).

30. Kantor's book is discussed in chapter 2. Harry Turtledove, *The Guns of the South* (New York: Ballantine, 1993).

31. The loss of Robert E. Lee to a separate Confederate States politics is a recurring situation in these counterfactuals. Kantor and Turtledove imagine "President" Lee beginning the process of gradual integration. Historian Roger L. Ransom, in *The Confederate States of America: What Might Have Been* (New York: W. W. Norton, 2005), imagines a scenario in which, by the 1880s, a victorious Confederacy achieves a kind of emancipation by buying out slaveholders' investments in their human property (197–207). Ransom also imagines bold presidential leadership in the separate CSA (201), although he names no names. He stops short, however, of imagining full racial harmony; freed blacks in his counterfactual CSA would still suffer as second-class social and economic inferiors to the whites. A similar murky inconclusiveness is the case in the counterfactual south of *Captain Confederacy.*

32. Fans of the television series *The West Wing* (NBC, 1999–2006) will remember that the fictional president of that political drama, acted by Martin Sheen, bore the name Josiah "Jed" Bartlet.

33. Among the more than twelve thousand Union troops killed in the Battle of Fredericksburg were many of the Irish Brigade recruited mostly from the Irish Catholics of New York.

34. A significant part of the diversion away from slavery has Colonel Robert Gould Shaw and the Fifty-Fourth Massachusetts Regiment transported by Gingrich and Forstchen out of the battle at Fort Wagner in South Carolina (where Shaw was killed and buried in a common grave with his dead African American troops) and arriving in Washington in the nick of time to help to repel this Confederate attack. Thus are Massachusetts and the Union deprived of a hero and Robert Lowell of the powerful subject matter of his centennial poem "For the Union Dead" (1960).

35. The Lincoln government, on May 22, 1863, issued General Order 143, creating the United States Colored Troops, to which Douglass responded with the often-quoted statement: "Once let the black man get upon his *person* the brass letter, U.S., let him get an eagle on his button, and a musket on his shoulder and bullets in his pocket, there is no power on earth that can deny that he has earned the right to citizenship."

36. Unlike Gingrich, who did serve as Speaker of the House of Representatives, Washburne was defeated in his attempt at that post. He did become Grant's secretary of state; he was not Lincoln's.

37. E. L. Doctorow, *The March* (New York: Random House, 2010).

38. Sartorious is a character in an earlier novel by Doctorow, *The Waterworks* (New York: Random House, 1994).

39. Of course Emily is correct. Doctorow had already conceived of Sartorious about a decade after his Civil War service, part of the financial-political-scientific combine of *The Waterworks*.

40. Doctorow's novel *Ragtime* (New York: Random House, 1975) focuses on the early twentieth-century winners and losers in the new urban, industrial economy. One of Doctorow's characters in *Ragtime*, Coalhouse Walker, a ragtime pianist in New York City, appears in name at least in *The March*. In *The March*, however, the character of that name persuades his wife, a former slave liberated by the march, to turn away from her dream of a life in a big northern city: "[F]orty acres of good loam and a plow and a mule and some seed. And with that I will make a life for us" (127). In the context of *The March,* this Coalhouse makes a poetically evocative but doomed choice.

Index

Page, Thomas Nelson, 98n18
Plessy v. Ferguson, 163 U.S. 537
    (1896), 2, 15
Portman, John, 66
Potter, David M., 102n7, 103n14

race suicide, 6–7, 9–11, 13, 23, 26
Ransom, Roger L., 105n31
Requiem for a Nun (Faulkner),
    x, 69
Rivers, Larry, 34
Road to Reunion, The (Buck),
    98–99n21
Romine, Scott, 76
Roosevelt, Theodore, 6–9, 14, 18

Selznick, David O., 32–33
Sheldon, Edward, 98n19; *The
    Governor*, 21–23; *The Nigger*,
    21
Shetterly, Will, 59–61, 68, 101n1
Sound and the Fury, The
    (Faulkner), 64
South Atlantic Modern Language
    Association (SAMLA), 67
Stephens, Alexander, 74–76

Stoddard, Lothrop, 96n3
Stoker, Bram, 4–6
Stone, Vince, 59–60, 68
Stowe, Harriet Beecher, 14, 18–20
Stribling, T. S., 67

Taft, William Howard, 2
Turtledove, Harry, 78, 105
Twain, Mark, 22
2000 Maniacs (Lewis), 71

Warren, Robert Penn, xi; *The
    Legacy of the Civil War*
    (1961), 30, 38–46, 49, 76, 88;
    Wilderness, 49–55
Whitman, Walt, 13, 71, 88
Wilderness (Warren), 49–55
Wilson, Edmund, 37–39, 44,
    100n18
Wilson, Woodrow, 2, 13–15, 23,
    26, 72, 97n13
Wolfe, Thomas, 67
Wolfe, Tom, 68
Woolson, Albert, 28–29, 31–32,
    36, 100n12

Selected Books from the Mercer University Lamar Memorial Lectures

꿏

The Brown *Decision, Jim Crow, and Southern Identity*
James C. Cobb

Teaching Equality: Black Schools in the Age of Jim Crow
Adam Fairclough

Becoming Confederates: Paths to a New National Loyalty
Gary W. Gallagher

*A Consuming Fire: The Fall of the Confederacy in the Mind
of the White Christian South*
Eugene D. Genovese

Moses, Jesus, and the Trickster in the Evangelical South
Paul Harvey

George Washington and the American Military Tradition
Don Higginbotham

South to the Future: An American Region in the Twenty-First Century
Edited by Fred Hobson

The Countercultural South
Jack Temple Kirby

A Late Encounter with the Civil War
Michael Kreyling

*Singing Cowboys and Musical Mountaineers: Southern Culture
and the Roots of Country Music*
Bill C. Malone

"Mixed Blood" Indians: Racial Construction in the Early South
Theda Perdue